The Financial Giants in United States History

The Financial Giants in United States History

STEPHEN GIRARD • JOHN JACOB ASTOR
JAY COOKE • DANIEL DREW
CORNELIUS VANDERBILT • JAY GOULD • JIM FISK

by
Meade Minnigerode

With 16 Illustrations

BeardBooks
Washington, DC

Copyright ©1926, 1927 by P. F. Collier & Son Co.
Reprinted 2003 by Beard Books

Copyright© 1927 by Meade Minnigerode

The original title of this work was
Certain Rich Men
The title has been changed to facilitate
electronic retrieval and/or to reflect
current conditions in the subject area.

ISBN 1-58798-149-1

Printed in the United States of America

By Meade Minnigerode

Laughing House
Oh, Susanna!
The Big Year
The Seven Hills
The Fabulous Forties, 1840-1850
Lives and Times
Aaron Burr—2 vols. (with Samuel H. **Wandell**)
Some American Ladies
Cordelia Chantrell
Certain Rich Men

For

ROBERT HOUSUM

CONTENTS

	PAGE
STEPHEN GIRARD	1
The Merchant Banker.	
JOHN JACOB ASTOR	31
The Fortune Maker.	
JAY COOKE	51
The Tycoon.	
DANIEL DREW	83
The Old Man of the Street.	
CORNELIUS VANDERBILT	101
The Commodore.	
JAY GOULD	135
The Wizard of Wall Street.	
JIM FISK	189
The Mountebank.	

GIRARD'S BANK
From a German engraving

ILLUSTRATIONS

	FACING PAGE
GIRARD'S BANK	*Frontispiece*
From a German engraving.	
STEPHEN GIRARD	12
From a painting by Chappel.	
GIRARD COLLEGE	24
From an engraving published in 1851.	
JOHN JACOB ASTOR	36
From a painting by Chappel.	
ASTORIA	46
JAY COOKE	62
From a photograph by Gutekunst, Philadelphia. Reproduced in *The Chronicles of America*, Yale University Press, Volume 41.	
A TIGHT DAY AT THE DISCOUNT DESK	76
From a contemporary print.	
DANIEL DREW	88
From an engraving by Buttre.	
THE HUDSON RIVER STEAMER "DREW"	98
Courtesy of the Robert Fridenberg Galleries.	
CORNELIUS VANDERBILT	110
THE STEAM YACHT "NORTH STAR"	128
From a contemporary woodcut.	

ILLUSTRATIONS

                                                                     FACING PAGE

JAY GOULD 142
    From an engraving by Hall.

SCENE IN THE GOLD ROOM ON BLACK FRIDAY . . 160
    From a woodcut in *Harper's Weekly*.

"RUINED" 180
    From a woodcut in *Harper's Weekly* inspired by Black Friday.

JAMES FISK, JR. 194

COLONEL JAMES FISK, JR. 206
    From the cover of the *Ninth Regiment Quickstep*.

BIBLIOGRAPHY

BIOGRAPHIES

H. W. Arey, *The Girard College and its Founder.*
N. W. Ayer, *In the Days of Stephen.*
J. F. Beale, see M. Halstead.
J. M. Beck, *Stephen Girard, Merchant and Mariner.*
G. S. Boutwell, *Reminiscences of Sixty Years in Public Affairs.*
E. L. Gebhard, *The Life and Ventures of the original John Jacob Astor.*
M. Halstead, with J. F. Beale, *Life of Jay Gould.*
B. J. Hendrick, *The Astor Fortune.*
B. J. Hendrick, *The Gould Fortune.*
B. J. Hendrick, *The Vanderbilt Fortune.*
A. C. Herrick, *Stephen Girard, Founder.*
H. A. Ingram, *The Life and Character of Stephen Girard.*
H. A. Ingram, *The Life of Jean Girard de Montbrun.*
Willoughby Jones, *Life of James Fisk, Jr.*
R. W. McAlpine, *The Life and Times of Colonel James Fisk, Jr.*
J. B. McMaster, *Life and Times of Stephen Girard.*
D. F. More, *History of the More Family.*
G. Myers, *History of the Great American Fortunes.*
H. D. Northrop, *Life and Achievements of Jay Gould.*

BIBLIOGRAPHY

E. P. Oberholtzer, *Jay Cooke, Financier of the Civil War.*
James Parton, *Famous Americans of Recent Times.*
James Parton, *Life of John Jacob Astor.*
W. E. Selleck, *Selleck Memorial (Gold Family).*
Trumbull White, *The Wizard of Wall Street and his Wealth.*

GENERAL

C. F. Adams, *Chapters of Erie and other Essays.*
Anonymous, *The Life of Colonel James Fisk, Jr., etc.*
Anonymous, *A Life of James Fisk, Jr., etc.*
Anonymous, *Romantic Incidents in the Life of James Fisk, Jr., etc.*
Walter Barrett, *The Merchants of Old New York.*
W. H. Bayles, *Old Taverns of New York.*
Stuart Daggett, *Railroad Reorganization.*
Delaney, *Song Book.*
F. E. Dayton, *Steamboat Days.*
C. H. Haswell, *Reminiscences of an Octogenarian.*
B. J. Hendrick, *The Age of Big Business.*
Philip Hone, *Diary.*
Washington Irving, *Astoria.*
William Leech, *Argument in proof of monomania in the case of Cornelius Vanderbilt, Deceased.*
J. B. McMaster, *History of the People of the United States.*
John Moody, *The Masters of Capital.*
John Moody, *The Railroad Builders.*
Putnams, *Historic New York.*
James Schouler, *History of the United States.*
W. O. Scroggs, *Filibusters and Financiers.*
C. L. Skinner, *Adventurers of Oregon.*
Bouck White, *The Book of Daniel Drew.*

NEWSPAPERS AND ARCHIVES

Congressional Globe, 1857–8, 1862–3.
House of Representatives, Forty-first Congress, Second Session, Report No. 31.
New York *Herald*, 1848, 1868–1870, 1872–3, 1877–8.
New York *Nation*, 1868–9.
New York *Sun*, 1877–8.
New York *Times*, 1877–8.
New York *Tribune*, 1869–1870, 1877–8.
New York *World*, 1877–8.

Certain Rich Men

Stephen Girard
The Merchant Banker

STEPHEN GIRARD

THE MERCHANT BANKER

1

"I THANK you for the prudent advice you give me," Stephen Girard once wrote to his brother, "but my love of work, the only pleasure I have on this globe, will not permit me to entertain these prudent considerations."

Work—the word is inseparable from the record of his career; the repetition of it runs like a thread through the whole tapestry of his life.

He was born on May 20, 1750, in a suburb of Bordeaux; the second child and oldest son of Odette Lafargue and Pierre Girard, retired naval officer, Cross of St. Louis for bravery, Captain of the Port. A respected sea-faring, merchant family. The boy was to have ten brothers and sisters, supplemented after 1767 by four half-brothers and sisters. His own mother he lost at the age of twelve; in after years he was not to remember ever having been able to see with his right eye; his education, he always rather bitterly maintained, had been neglected by his parents; at the age of fourteen, in 1764—before his father's second marriage, and consequently not as the alleged result of his dislike for his step-mother, which only developed later—he went to sea as a cabin boy. A cabin boy who owned a venture in the ship, furnished by his father. He made several voyages to Santo Domingo, became an officer, received his master's license, and in 1774 sailed away once more, never to return. His own venture in the voyage turned out disastrously; he was in debt to several merchants in Bordeaux; except for his brother Jean, he was never again to see his brothers and sisters or his father.

He obtained his discharge from the ship; in July, 1774, he landed in New York, and was employed as mate and captain by the firm of Thomas Randall and Son; and finally one day in June, 1776, he found himself in Philadelphia—wondering, perhaps, what all the excitement over the Continental Congress might signify. The capture of New York by the British brought Thomas Randall to Philadelphia, and there for a few months Mr. Randall, and Isaac Hazlehurst, and Stephen conducted a precarious business with the West Indies. But the British cruisers were making commerce impossible, and in 1777 Stephen turned for a while to the wholesale buying and selling of general merchandise. And he made some money, for although the Bordeaux merchants were not all paid, he purchased a small estate at Mount Holly, in New

Jersey—the domestic reason for this step will presently be made clear—and he purchased, or built, the sloop *Water Witch,* only to have her seized by the British. He was twenty-eight, and he was already very busy.

2

He rented a store in North Water Street—he was to live in that same street for some fifty years—and continued his general merchandising; he took the oath of allegiance and, in 1779, became an American citizen; he began to pester his brother Jean, who was now at The Cape in Santo Domingo, for consignments of syrup and salt; he engaged in various unsuccessful privateering enterprises; and in 1780 he formed a partnership with a certain Captain Baldesqui, and established the maritime firm of Stephen Girard and Company, to which he was able now—of course some of the Bordeaux creditors were not yet paid—to contribute 10,000 *livres*. The firm met with some success—the brig *Flora,* for instance, fought and captured "a charming ship . . . loaded with Madeira wine and gin"—but the times were perilous, prices were high, and currency unstable. "May the devil carry off all the paper money," the Captain wrote, "and the people who invented it!" As for the British, "may hell confound them!" In general, "it appears that we are not lucky in our ventures."

Perhaps the real trouble was that Captain Baldesqui was not a prudent man of affairs, not successful enough in securing new business. As Stephen remarked, in Santo Domingo he had "not procured any commissions . . . the profits arising from which could purchase a tooth picker." In fact, Stephen wished him to retire from the firm "to which he was never of the least utility." At all events, in 1782, the partnership was dissolved, with attendant disputes finally arbitrated in Stephen's favor.

3

Stephen soon after built the brig *The Two Brothers* and placed her in the Santo Domingo trade, consigned to his brother Jean. A curious trade, complicated with restrictions, and embargoes, and subterfuges, in which the two living brothers showed themselves to be cunning avoiders of the law. Flour must never appear on the manifest, because its importation was forbidden by the French; sugar and coffee might not be taken out, and so the ship must always carry a great deal of "lumber"; when ports were closed the brig must put in "by accident"; contraband cargoes had frequently to be taken on at sea from barges; it was often necessary to prevaricate concerning the ownership of vessels; captains were sometimes obliged —their sealed orders so informed them—to change their destination because of "stress of weather." But it could not be helped, everyone was doing the same, and there were great profits to be made.

Although Stephen was not always satisfied. "It is amusing to have you ask me how you can make more money," Jean wrote to him. "You will always be the same—never content." And he was inclined to false economies, Jean complained, mixing in poor flour with good. Jean complained a great deal, and upbraided Stephen for "those adventures which I have always detested and which you persist in undertaking"; but not so long before he had been writing that "would to God . . . you had ordered a barrel of flour to be placed in each hogshead of rice, without the knowledge of the crew"; and in 1786 he had finally entered into a partnership with his brother, Sn. and Jn. Girard, which lasted until 1790, and brought Jean to Philadelphia to manage affairs while Stephen was away on his one voyage to Marseilles, where he formed a business connection of long duration with Samatan Brothers.

The breaking up of the partnership was followed by a long dispute, involving sums which Jean maintained were due him and a bitter exchange of accusations, until Jean finally threatened to inform against some of Stephen's illegal transactions unless he were paid. "What was to be done in such a contingency?" Stephen's agents exclaimed. They paid, and Stephen wrote to his sister concerning Jean that he had resolved "not to think of him any longer. I shall say about him what my late father said"—Pierre Girard had recently died, leaving an estate hopelessly entangled in family and creditors' litigation—"that he is a worthless fellow who is not to be trusted. . . . You may tell him what I said if you ever see him." Perhaps Stephen also resented having Jean write to him that "this is not the time to make money on loans with large discounts, as you have made most of your money"—and some of those Bordeaux merchants still waiting to be paid. But it was not long before Jean was back in Philadelphia with his family; the two brothers became friends again; and for several years until he acquired his own ship Jean served as supercargo in Girard vessels. And Stephen bought a wreck and refitted her, and named her *The Good Friends* in honor of the reconciliation; and until her capture during the war of 1812 she remained "that favorite vessel" in his thoughts.

4

Loans with large discounts, "as you have made most of your money"—contraband cargoes—whatever it was, Stephen was acquiring a fortune. It was in 1790, he was forty years old, perhaps one had better begin calling him Mr. Girard. The ships were going back and forth, to Marseilles, to Santo Domingo—wheat, lumber, flour, fish, molasses, sugar, coffee;

he moved into a new house and counting room, on the old street; he built some more ships, the *Sally*, the *Liberty*, the *Voltaire* which always sailed from her home port on a Friday, just to show that Mr. Girard was not superstitious. Sometimes he lost $30,000 on a cargo; at other times he cleared as much as $100,000 on a single successful voyage. Some ten years later, in 1803, he could write to Mr. Gallatin that—

"I have three ships with their cargoes at sea, on their voyages to India. . . . I have a ship building . . . and another ship in this port . . . from Russia. . . . I own also two-fifths of the ship Fanny and cargo . . . from Sumatra. . . . To this I may add the goods which I have on hand, my real estate and outstanding debts, and about $40,000 . . . stock. The cargoes . . . which I have at sea . . . amounting together to $464,418 71/100 without . . . the value of my ships which . . . could not be purchased for $100,000."

And a part of the outstanding debts was a mere £60,000 sterling owed him in London. A considerable inventory for the one time cabin boy.

Especially when one recalls the circumstances under which the business was conducted, the growing business which took his ships all over Europe, to Russia, to China and to the Indies. The French Revolution, "John Adams's war" with France, the slave insurrections in Santo Domingo, the Napoleonic upheavals; decrees, orders in council, embargoes, blockades, privateers; detentions, seizures, claims, protests, sequestrations—it is not feasible in these pages to give any account of these endless vexations; one must turn to Professor McMaster's *Life* in order to follow them through many agitated chapters of ceaseless worry, from the days of 1790 right up to the American Long Embargo of 1808 and 1809, when Mr. Girard saw all his ships laid up for months; the *Voltaire,* the *Good Friends,* the *Liberty* and the *Montesquieu* at Gloucester Point, the *Helvetius* and the *Rousseau* at their own dock. The Long "Dambargo" as the Federalists called it; and while Mr. Girard was no Federalist, but a strong Jeffersonian Republican, still he probably agreed with them in this case, for if there was one thing that pained him it was to see beautiful ships lying idle. He obeyed the laws, though. None of that spurious "coastwise" trade—and then turn up in Havana after being "blown out" of your course—for him. The old Santo Domingo days were over.

He waited patiently; he took his losses with his profits, without batting his one good left eyelid; he always found "everything for the best, as Panglos says" —one of his favorite expressions—and whenever they would let him he sent out his ships again, to such "permitted ports" as might be open, to the Baltic, to Mocha, to South America, to Canton, to the Isle de

France—any place where there was a dock, and some bales of goods to be loaded and taken somewhere else. A valiant American merchant mariner.

5

Sometimes there was serious trouble.

In 1803, when Barclay and Company failed in London, and drafts of theirs amounting to £45,000 which Mr. Girard had sold to the United States came due. Mr. Gallatin had to insist, and Mr. Girard lost some $24,000 before the transaction was cleared up; but he was the gainer from it too, for it brought him to an association with the London firm of Baring which endured for twenty-eight years.

And in 1812, when in expectation of the raising of the Non Importation embargo against England, Mr. Girard loaded his *Good Friends* with English goods to the value of some £67,000 representing *a part* of his balance at Baring's, and sent her to the Spanish Amelia Island in Florida to await developments. But when she arrived there had been an uprising and Amelia was American, and the ship's status under the Act was somewhat dubious. The American commander allowed her to proceed to Philadelphia, but at Wilmington the United States customs libelled her. Mr. Girard retained Cæsar Rodney, and the ship was released fast enough, but the Federal Treasury decided that the double duty and other penalties under the Act must be paid. The total sum required was $900,000. Mr. Rodney of course appealed, and in 1819, after several anxious petitions to Congress, the case was finally settled for some $53,000 only. But the *Good Friends* was then no longer a Girard ship. "That favorite vessel" had been captured during the English war; and while the Barings bought her back, following Mr. Girard's instructions, the British authorities refused her clearance, and after the peace it was not possible to secure American registry for her again. Mr. Girard had no insurance on either ship or cargo—this seems to have frequently been the case with him—and "it will teach me to be more prudent," he remarked.

And the *Montesquieu* had been captured, captured and ransomed for $180,000. But in this case, considering the times, Mr. Girard cannot be said to have been unduly unfortunate. On the plea of his ransom loss he did his best without success to persuade Congress to remit his cargo dues. But after all, while the cargo was not worth the million and a half dollars estimated by the newspapers, still it sold for nearly $490,000. Including the ransom, the venture was well on the credit side of the ledger, and the ship was saved to continue her voyages until she was wrecked in 1824, two years after the loss of the uninsured *Voltaire*.

And after the peace with England, and more par-

From a painting by Chappel

ticularly after Waterloo, there was little profit on incoming cargoes. Outgoing voyages were lucrative enough, $70,000, $100,000, but homeward bound the ships brought little else besides specie. But Mr. Girard kept them moving, especially to the Far East, although in the late 1820s the losses were constantly increasing. "The present commercial prospect . . . of the United States is very discouraging," he wrote in 1826, "and was it not that the sole pleasure and amusement which I enjoy is to be constantly busy in following my usual occupations, I would have quit business long ago." That was it, he must be constantly busy, and his ships must never be idle. "As to profit, I do not expect any."

Some of the vessels were at sea, still carrying his flag, when he died, in 1831.

6

He was a great merchant, a great lover of ships, a great employer of men. He conducted mercantile operations on a world-wide scale and was acquainted with every local detail of his business; he exacted every last relentless penny from his contracts and pocketed losses of thousands of dollars without any dismay. If he was close fisted he was never niggardly. Considering his beginnings, the prolonged maritime unrest of his period and the modest roster of his fleet—of the eighteen vessels which he owned he never operated more than six at any one time—he was one of the greatest merchant mariners America has ever known. A sailor, a licensed captain, a trader to his marrow, shrewd, industrious and daring. Of course they called him lucky.

But "no man perhaps ever possessed so great and perfect a genius for trade and commerce," one of his clerks said of him. Not only a superficial cunning in speculation,

"but that sound penetration and various knowledge of the products of countries and the state of markets, the seasons and climates . . . which constitute . . . the mental chart of the intelligent, talented and liberal merchant; combined with a constant observation of the political and domestic situation of countries."

He was very just, he never scolded, he had no patience with stupidity, but he forgave mistakes. Of the men and boys around him he required honesty, punctuality and sober habits—he would not have drunkards on his ships, and so instructed his captains, or any man who made himself obnoxious to the rest—and above all he required obedience. Absolute, unquestioning obedience to his wishes. "Break owners, not orders" was the unchanging rule of the establishment. The supercargo who saved his ship from capture, or doubled his profits by disregarding orders was felicitated and dismissed. Mr.

Girard's apprentices were all sons of merchants and gentlemen, they were accepted free out of friendship, in most cases, for their fathers, they were often received in their employer's home and regaled with fruit from his farm, they were not allowed to gossip outside concerning counting house affairs, and they were expected to go to church on Sundays. Did they deserve it—and he was an excellent judge—they enjoyed Mr. Girard's trust to a degree considered quite unusual; when they grew up they became supercargoes and confidential clerks; and by some of them, at least, he was looked upon and venerated as a benefactor and friend. Gazing at the four chairs, at the one walnut and the three pine desks in the plain, unpretentious counting room on North Water Street, the public probably failed to appreciate these matters which it had perhaps already made up its mind to disbelieve.

It was a sturdy fleet—"charming ships"—a great house known around the world, the owner of which was able "to sell my goods on credit and to carry on my maritime business throughout cash in hand, without the aid of a discount. All this I owe principally to my close attention to business and to the resources which this fine country affords to all active or industrious men." Work, "the only pleasure I have on this globe"—that was the secret.

He accumulated enormous sums of money—his

funds in London alone, "locked up in the hands of Messrs. Baring Brothers" in 1811, amounted to nearly £195,000—with John Jacob Astor he was probably the wealthiest man of his day in the country. It may, on a subsequent page, be of value to learn what he did with all this money; to contemplate the tragedy of his private life from which his love of work may perhaps have been the only possible refuge.

7

Making money "on loans with large discounts, as you have made most of your money"—it was back in the 1780s that Jean Girard had written that to his brother Stephen. Maybe so, at all events the enterprises of banking were probably always a part of Mr. Girard's activities; and in 1812—when the State Legislature had refused to charter the defunct Bank of the United States—Mr. Girard gathered together a million dollars or so of his available funds, purchased the former United States Bank building and "having," as he informed the Barings,

"in several instances experienced that the magnitude of the funds . . . employed in my maritime commerce has induced me to make hazardous shipments, I have judged advisable to establish a private bank."

Stephen Girard's Bank, for the transaction of business "on my private account . . . as far as prudence will permit."

Naturally "the banks of this city do not appear friendly to my establishment although I take their notes . . . yet they uniformly refuse to take my bank notes." And there were other troubles. The Legislature considered an act forbidding private banking; Congress established stamp duties on notes injurious to the private banker; there were memorials, petitions and vetoes; in 1814, during the English war—when Mr. Girard was transporting all of his movable property to safe hiding places in the country—the banks suspended specie payments and he found himself sued by various individuals; but in 1815 he was able to say that his bank capital exceeded $1,800,000, and at his death its property was worth some $4,848,000. In his bedroom, where he must inevitably see it as soon as he opened his one good eye, hung a small print of his "little institution."

8

And now Mr. Girard really began to use his money.

In March, 1813, the Federal Treasury, facing bankruptcy, opened subscription books in various cities for a government loan of $16,000,000. The American nation, and very reluctantly, subscribed some $6,000,000 only. Mr. Gallatin having invited proposals from individuals for disposing of the balance on a commission basis, David Parish brought John Jacob Astor and Mr. Girard together, and between them they subscribed for the remaining $10,000,000, Mr. Girard's and Mr. Parish's share amounting to $7,055,800, at $88 for each hundred dollar certificate.

The other banks considered this an excellent opportunity to embarrass Mr. Girard, and began presenting Treasury drafts for specie, contrary to the agreement with Government. But when the Bank of Pennsylvania demanded $15,000 in specie, Mr. Girard sent around $300,000 worth of their own notes with a similar request. He did not propose to retain their notes "as a relick," and since other banks refused to take his notes and invariably presented them for specie payment, "why should I not [have] the same privilege when I have a similar credit on them?"

Precisely, and the result was that the Philadelphia banks finally decided to accept his notes.

And then in 1814 the state of the national currency was so deplorable that Congress determined to charter the second Bank of the United States. Mr. Astor wanted the parent bank in New York and Mr. Girard said it must be in Philadelphia, and after long Congressional discussions the new national bank was established in Philadelphia in 1816. Mr. Girard was appointed one of the five Government Directors, and when the public subscription books showed a deficit of more than $3,000,000, Mr. Girard immediately subscribed for the whole amount, in order "to promote the early operation of that indispensable institution," and to "prevent the increase of a multiplicity of proxies" which would "give more votes to thirty-one shares than to those who owned upwards of twenty thousand."

$3,083,000, on top of the 1813 loan—it made a sensation. People began to realize that Mr. Girard was extremely wealthy. These were public spirited, however profitable transactions—and, at that, the national bank shares began to drop almost immediately because, in his opinion, of "intrigue and corruption" among the elected directors. Transactions of national importance; but one admires him most, somehow, lending $100,000, in 1829, to save the Commonwealth of Pennsylvania from bankruptcy, to the Governor in person pending the convening of the Legislature which might or might not approve the loan.

9

And Mr. Girard had been using his money in other ways.

He had been investing in various enterprises for internal development—a subject which always claimed his interest—and all through the years he was purchasing real estate and improving it, erecting fine, solid houses which he planned himself. Farm lands, city blocks and buildings on Spruce, Front and Water Streets, on Second, Third and Fifth, and the block bounded by Market and Chestnut, and Eleventh and Twelfth; tracts in Kentucky, and some two hundred thousand acres of the old Bastrop Grant on the Wachita—where once Colonel Burr had hoped to found a colony; and coal lands in Schuylkill County, to serve which he was, at the time of his death, organizing the Danville and Pottsville Railroad to which he had subscribed $100,000.

Ships, banks, railroads, properties.

And of course, since he had so much money—his fortune was estimated, and quite incorrectly, at $40,000,000—every Tom, Dick and Harry in the country had something to suggest to Mr. Girard regarding the use which he might make of it. One individual had been instructed by "the Supreme Being" to ask Mr. Girard for $25,000; another hoped that he would finance a polar expedition to explore "the concave interior of this sphere"; still another that he would provide for "sending forth missionaries to the heathen"; a lady reminded him that "alms cover a multitude of sins"—not a very tactful insinuation perhaps; a quite spurious relative announced her desire to come and live, at his expense, in his home; and two enterprising gentlemen had everything arranged to kidnap him when they were arrested.

Even Mr. Monroe, during his second term as President, applied to Mr. Girard for the loan of twenty-five to forty thousand dollars for five years—something to do, perhaps, with the financial distress in which Mr. Monroe found himself because of the confusion in the accounts covering his grandiose refurnishing of the White House.

But Mr. Girard knew exactly what to do with his money. At his death it was discovered that he had bequeathed—in addition to various smaller gifts and annuities—some $300,000 to his relatives, to his captains and clerks, and to a number of benevolent institutions; $300,000 to the Commonwealth for canals; $500,000 to the City for the improvement of the Delaware front; and about $5,500,000, together with the necessary land, for the founding of a college for "poor male white orphan children." They were not to wear any distinctive dress; they were to be taught "facts and things rather than words or signs," and a "pure attachment to our Republican institutions"; and "no ecclesiastic, missionary or minister of any sect whatsoever" was ever to be admitted, even as a visitor. And the reason was that "the tender minds" of the orphans were to be kept free from "the excitements which clashing doctrines and sectarian controversy are apt to produce." When they grew up the orphans might adopt "such religious tenets as their mature reason may enable them to prefer."

In this manner did Mr. Girard dispose of his estate of nearly $7,000,000—to the great annoyance of his relatives who did their best to break the will.

10

His contemporaries really knew very little about him, and posterity has embroidered upon that ignorance. He was heavily built and stocky, he had only one eye, he spoke English very badly and occasionally displayed a violent temper—and so he was ungracious and repellent. Because he wore plain and scrupulously tidy broadcloth of the very best material, but always in the old "shadbelly" style, he was shabby and unimpressive, and they forgot the pair of shoes for every day in the week—he was always a great walker, which was the reason why he only kept a gig and not a carriage—and the silk underwear imported from China.

Because he hated waste, and extravagance, and ostentation, and because he always lived in a dingy part of town—near his ships—he was stingy, and crabbed, and unsocial; and yet his house was substantial and elegantly furnished; it possessed a copper roof and a marble floor, open coal fires and a bathroom—something which most Philadelphia mansions could not boast—his table was always well provided with luxuries, wine and fruit, and made itself frequently hospitable to the apprentices as well as to the French noble refugees of 1815, Grouchy, and the Lallemand brothers, and Joseph Bonaparte, who dined at his board with grateful regularity; its chambers were garnished with china and furniture from Bordeaux, black ebony and crimson velvet plush, there were marble statues and a mechanical organ, and in his own room he had a series of colored prints of Santo Domingo negresses.

He loved children, and especially orphans, and horses, dogs and singing birds—he had watch dogs on all his ships, and kept canaries in his home and in his private counting room which he taught to sing with a special bird organ—and in cold winters he gave away firewood to the poor. Of course he liked Voltaire and Rousseau, and named ships after them, and kept their books in his little library—and so he was irreligious if not an atheist; and yet he died in the Catholic church, he was a great admirer of the Quakers, he contributed repeatedly to religious enterprises of all denominations, he maintained a pew for his household and he required attendance in church every Sunday of his apprentices.

It is true that after Jean's death in 1803 he allowed his widow, whom he detested, to shift for herself and perish in poverty, and consequently he was a mean curmudgeon—but people did not remember that he had redeemed her silver, paid her debts and given her a small monthly allowance, and that he took her three little girls into his home and educated them, pending the long deferred settlement of their father's estate and debts; people did not recall that he had sent for two of his nephews from France when their father could no longer support them; people did not know that he had several times come to the assistance of his relatives in Bordeaux, to an extent which was "ten times more than I received . . . from my father, to whom I had no other obligation than that of having forced me to leave home in my youth, and seek my fortune in foreign countries where my good conduct, activity and love of work have placed me in a situation which merits the approval of my fellow citizens." A disgruntled generosity, perhaps, and he always counted his pennies, but the purse was open, and he had worked hard for his prosperity.

11

And people forgot another thing. They called Stephen Girard a mean, hard man, selfish, and scornful of his fellow beings, and in many ways he probably was. But they were forgetting, they had almost immediately forgotten.

In 1793—as again in 1797, in 1798, 1802 and in

GIRARD COLLEGE
From an engraving published in 1851

1820—Philadelphia was swept by the yellow fever. The horrors of those epidemics are too well known —the pest houses, the barricades, the informers and "inspectors," the pitiful methods of prevention, camphor and garlic, burning pitch, bonfires and gunpowder, airless rooms and bleeding—the panic of a population flying to the banks of the Schuylkill, the sufferings of the poor who could not afford to leave. Mr. Girard did not like doctors; he always considered himself "in the treatment of fevers, cuts, sores . . . as competent as anyone in the United States"; he insisted stoutly on all occasions that the epidemic was imaginary, caused by the alarming prognostications of "our infamous esculapians," and that it was fear which made the people ill; even in the terrible days of 1797 "we have not the slightest sign of an epidemic." But in 1793—he did similar work again in 1797 and 1798—he volunteered his services, and with Peter Helm and John Deveze was placed in charge of the Bush Hill pest house.

"The deplorable condition . . . of our city," he wrote, "claims the aid of all those who are not afraid of death . . . I shall accordingly be very busy . . . and if I have the misfortune to be overcome by the fatigue of my labors I shall have the satisfaction of having performed a duty which we owe to one another." And anyway, Frenchmen "do not die easily."

For two months he and his companions were in attendance at the pest house every day, "and not only saw that the nurses did their duties, but they actually performed many of the most dangerous and at the same time humiliating services for the sick with their own hands." It was often difficult to make the patients swallow the nauseating medicines, and Mr. Girard persuaded them with infinite patience, subjecting himself to the most revolting accidents. "It is a proof of the kindness of your heart," a friend wrote to him, but "you are not the only one on the committee, and each member might take his turn." At the end of it all the City of Philadelphia gave him a handsome resolution of thanks.

Her citizens might well in future years have cherished more warmly the recollection of a not insignificant act of great-hearted courage, humanity and devotion. Of course, after the will had been read, they, in turn, gave him a handsome funeral.

And there was still something else that people forgot. Something to account for his aloofness, for his lack of gaiety and geniality, for his concentration on business in which men would see only a passion for making money.

He had, in 1777, married a young girl of sixteen named Mary Lumm. It was for her that the little estate at Mount Holly had been purchased. "Tired of the risks of a sailor's life and accompanying libertinage without religious control," he told his father, "I determined to settle ashore . . . I have taken a wife who is without fortune, it is true, but whom I love and with whom I am living very happily." She was beautiful, she had lovely black hair, she was the daughter of a ship builder—Mr. Parton will have it that she was a barefoot servant girl at the town pump—she had very little education or refinement, she was very much beneath her husband in station. There it was. He married her; and while brother Jean did not like her at all at first, he came in time to be very fond of her. In 1785 she went insane.

"I presume," Jean wrote, "that the grief which this lovely woman has always shown to me at having no children is the cause of her misfortune." The husband was distracted; "I fear that I have lost for ever the peace which a certain success should procure for life in this world"; he suffered "so much crushing grief in silence that my health has become greatly enfeebled." They put her in the Pennsylvania Hospital; after a while she seemed better and came home; but in 1790 she had to go back again. Early in 1791 she gave birth to a daughter who died a few months later. In 1815 she herself expired, at the Hospital. "It is very well," Mr. Girard said as he stood by her grave.

12

Is it so very remarkable that he should have turned from all this to his ships, to his counting house, to his bank, to his beloved farm?

"The sole amusement which I enjoy," he wrote in later years, "is to be in the country constantly busy in attending to the work of the farm generally, also to my fruit trees, several of which, say about three hundred, I have imported from France, and I hope will be useful to our country. In addition to that I have two extensive gardens, the whole of which I direct throughout. . . . All my valuable fruit trees are uniformly planted or trained by me. . . . If you want some good [vegetable] seed please to let me know it. I raise it myself, from seed which I received . . . from . . . Europe, consequently it is pretty good. . . . I have taken much pains with grape vines."

Grapes, plums and pigs were his specialty, and vegetables since in his old age he gave up meat entirely—but not his favorite cider, and his spoonful of Holland gin in the afternoon, and his fearfully strong, unsweetened black coffee. He went to the farm every day; his produce and stock were sent to the Philadelphia markets; and a month before he died he said "when death comes for me he will find me busy, unless I am asleep. If I thought I was going to die tomorrow, I should nevertheless plant a tree today."

And he went to his counting room and to his bank, every day until the last brief attack of pneumonia, that "violent" and "extraordinary disorder"—except for two months in 1831, after he had been run over in the street and painfully injured about the head—keeping up the old habits, arising very early in the morning and "often before break of day," this restless, lonely gentleman of eighty.

He had to keep busy, "labor is the price of life, its happiness, its everything; to rest is to rust; every man should labor to the last hour of his ability." Of course he was ambitious, he would never be content Jean had told him, he enjoyed the power which money brought him, he preferred things to people, he took pride in his possessions; but "I do not value fortune. The love of labor is my highest ambition."

The love of labor—but surely there was another incentive. This childless man who loved children so much, married for twenty-five years to a wife who sat staring emptily out of a hospital window, he must have tried to forget, to bury himself, to find in strenuous industry some substitute for that "peace which a certain success should procure for life in this world," and which had been denied him. He must keep busy; leisure of thought was for him the opened door to a chamber of sorrow and regrets; with his necessarily slender intellectual resources, his dislike of social folderol, his indifference to politics—they had made him serve as Selectman and Port Warden—the counting room was the only place. There, at his plain desk, with the canaries chirping in their brass cages, he found contentment.

This man who, it is said, confessed once that he worked all day so that he might sleep at night.

John Jacob Astor
The Fortune Maker

JOHN JACOB ASTOR

THE FORTUNE MAKER

1

THE butcher, the baker, the fortune maker . . .

"Your old friend Mr. Astor is very feeble," Mr. McKenney wrote to Mrs. Madison in 1846, and he "can have no pleasure in life. I am told by those who best know him that his relish for wealth is as keen as ever; that gone, he is gone."

He was born on July 17, 1763, in the village of Waldorf in Germany, the youngest of four sons of Jacob Astor, or Ashdor, a convivially spendthrift butcher of that place. As soon as they could, the three older sons abandoned the paternal shop, taking with them those habits of frugality and industry which they had inherited from their mother, and sought their fortunes elsewhere—George in London, where he became a partner with an uncle in the firm of Astor and Broadwood, makers of musical instruments; Henry in America, at first perhaps with the Hessians, and subsequently as a rising butcher in the Fly Market at New York; John Melchior as the steward of a German noble's estate. John Jacob, the youngest, was left at home to mind the shop, a ragged, hungry, unhappy boy who ran away sometimes to the neighbors in order to escape from his stepmother's tantrums.

And finally, early in the 1780s, he persuaded his father to give him a few crowns, and he too went away from Waldorf. On foot to the Rhine, and then on lumber rafts down the river, and so at last to London where his brother found employment for him in the musical instrument workshop. He had "a clear head," his village schoolmaster had said of him, "and everything right behind the ears." And he was healthy and enormously persevering. He learned English and saved money. Fifteen precious guineas, after two or three grinding years, with which he purchased seven German flutes as a stock in trade, and a steerage passage to America. In November, 1783, he sailed for Baltimore; a long, stormy crossing, and at the end of it the ship was held by the ice for weeks in the Chesapeake Bay. But there was a young German aboard who was occupied in the fur trade, and from him John Jacob secured much engrossing information concerning this lucrative traffic.

In March, 1784, the ice broke up; he went ashore in Baltimore and made his way to New York, to brother Henry's, armed with his seven German flutes, and an idea revolving in his mind.

2

The chronology of these years is a little uncertain. Brother Henry received him kindly; for a while he peddled cakes for baker Diederich; soon he was taken into Robert Bowne's fur store and set to beating furs to keep out the moths. He was quick to learn, he was always questioning the Indians, and he came to love the sight and feel of fine skins. It was not long before he was being sent as a buyer to Montreal, and proving himself a shrewd, hard bargain driver. Some two years later, he was able to enter the trade on his own account; he opened a little shop on Water Street, toys, gimcracks and peltries; he travelled constantly all over New York State collecting skins; he married Sarah Todd and found in her an enthusiastic and competent judge of furs. As soon as possible, he took a consignment over to London, sold it at a good profit, and returned to New York with the agency for his brother's violins, flutes and pianos. In his new store on Gold Street he sold "Furs and Pianos."

In 1790, he was a "Fur Trader," in 1794, a "Furrier," in 1796 a "Fur Merchant" on Broadway. He had a ship carrying his goods to London, and made several voyages himself; he went frequently to Montreal to purchase from the North West Company, and employed an increasing number of trappers; he was making money—and so was brother Henry, who had a habit of riding out of town and buying up the incoming droves of cattle, to the great annoyance of his less energetic colleagues who objected to his "forestalling" and protested to the Common Council concerning what they considered his "pernicious practices." But Henry Astor, or Ashdor, was not disturbed; he married the pretty daughter of a brother butcher, and called her "de pink of de Powery"; he owned the Bull's Head Tavern property; he put his accumulating profits into real estate and told John Jacob to do the same.

In 1800 the immigrant boy was worth some $250,000, and sent his first ship to Canton. After that it was easy; furs to London and Canton, and return cargoes of Chinese merchandise and tea. And the Government helped, for China merchants did not have to pay their import duties for as much as a year after entry—a sort of government loan without interest. And in John Jacob Astor's case the Government seems to have helped in other ways; for in 1808, during the Long Embargo, his *Beaver* was allowed to sail when no other "sea letter" ships were moving. No one knew why, and when it was rumored that he had received permission to take a Chinese Mandarin home, the merchants insisted that it was a hoax and that Mr. Astor had picked up a stray Chinaman on the wharves.

From a painting by Chappel

Little by little, he was acquiring a fortune. No one realized this, he lived so quietly, so economically, so stingily it was thought by many. He had his first million, he recalled in later years, before anyone suspected it. The butcher, the baker, the fortune maker.

3

And in the North, at the Beaver Club on Beaver Hall Hill in Montreal, and especially at Fort William on Lake Superior, in the great council room and banqueting hall hung with Indian trophies, the magnates of the North West Fur Company—those proud *Hommes du Nord* from the *Pays d'En Haut*, the "top country" bordering on the Arctic—were assembling in annual state for parliaments of the company partners, to discuss the policies of the association, and feast on buffalo tongue and beaver tail served in silver platters marked with the company beaver crest and motto—Fortitude in Distress.

Canada had been English since 1763, and the Company of the Adventurers of England Trading into Hudson's Bay—since 1670—had been restored to power. But the old French fur trade, the wide ranging forest trade of the singing *voyageurs* and *coureurs-de-bois*, was dead. In their place, had come the "free traders," and an era of violence and lawless competition, resulting in the formation, in 1779, of the Michilimackinac Company, the "Mackinaws"; and, in 1783, of the Montreal North West Company —the disdainful, arrogant, magnificently self-confident "Nor'westers"; Scotch Highlanders, most of them, McTavishes, McKensies, McDougals and McDonalds; young men, bold men, violent men, and old *coureurs-de-bois* and *voyageurs,* animated by a clan spirit of intense loyalty, swinging through the territory of the rival Mackinaws with jaunty feathers in their caps, and Nor'wester badges on their beaded shirts ornamented with bells and fringes, and restless fingers playing about the handles of loosely sheathed dirks.

And to Fort William they came in all their finery, as to a gathering of the Highland clans; partners from the outlying posts with their trappers and Indians; partners from Montreal, bejewelled and befurred, in long canoes bearing bakers and cooks, delicacies and vintage wines; each with his "brigade" of singing *voyageurs*. They came to sit in prosperous conclaves; to dine with toasts and bumpers in glittering, gold braided uniforms; to sing the songs of Scotland and of the great northern woods, and to watch the Indian dances and hear the old *chansons* at the *régale* of their retainers; to get, no doubt, most royally drunk. Fortitude in Distress.

And during the long intervening months, they carried on the trade, they explored, they spread the boundaries of the North West Company. Alexander McKenzie, Alexander Mackay, David Thompson, the Indians' "Star Man." They knew the country from the Great Lakes to the Rockies, they had seen the Pacific, they had reached the Arctic. They remembered that an American ship captain, in 1792, had found the mouth of the legendary River of the West, the Columbia, and that an American fur trade with Canton was expanding out there; they were watching the Russians' little game at New Archangel in Alaska; in 1805, they realized that Meriwether Lewis and William Clark, Americans again, had gone overland to the western River and followed it to the ocean. They understood all these things, and pondered them. From the Great Lakes to the Pacific—one feather, perhaps, one badge, one company? Before it was too late? One motto? Fortitude in Distress.

4

And in New York, Mr. Astor also understood all these things, and pondered them. No feathers and badges for him, perhaps—no such extravagance—but from the Great Lakes to the Pacific, one company, one flag? The American flag. A chain of posts across the plains, trading settlements on the Columbia, an arrangement with the Russians to accomplish which he sent an agent to St. Petersburg,

American ships to carry the peltries to Canton, and the whole continental fur trade in American hands. And while there was involved the possibility of immense profits, it was not that alone. He really, for once in his life, seems to have seen a vision and dreamed a dream. Expansion, colonization, national commerce. And the Government heartily approved;

"I considered," Mr. Jefferson wrote, "as a great public acquisition, the commencement of a settlement on that point of the western coast of America, and looked forward with gratification to the time when its descendants should have spread themselves through the whole length of that coast. . . . " But of course "the executive could give no direct aid."

In 1808, Mr. Astor had already founded the American Fur Company. Then, with the Nor'westers, he had bought out the Mackinaws, receiving their Wisconsin posts as his share and merging his two enterprises into the South West Company. Now, in 1810, he suggested that the Nor'westers join him and take a one-third interest in his new Pacific venture. But the Nor'westers had other beavers to skin. They were planning a descent of their own on the Columbia, they had ordered exploration in that region with a view to acquiring a charter from the British Government, they did not desire to see the Pacific coast overrun with Astor men. They declined

Mr. Astor's proposal, and said nothing. But they sent David Thompson to the Columbia.

Mr. Astor went ahead with his plans. A ship, the *Tonquin*, to sail to the mouth of the Columbia and found a settlement; an expedition to go up the Missouri, and then overland to the new post. In June, 1810, the Pacific Fur Company articles were signed; Mr. Astor had been recruiting in Canada, from the Nor'wester ranks themselves—such men as Ross, Franchère, the Stuarts, Duncan McDougal, Alexander Mackay; in September, the *Tonquin* sailed, under the command of Captain Thorn, a well meaning, utterly tactless martinet who despised his passengers—the Scotch partners, and the bragging, roistering, gaudy Canadian trappers and *coureurs* whose temperament he so little understood. And they hated him, and annoyed him in every possible way, and talked among themselves in Gaelic so that he saw "conspiracies" behind every door. And perhaps he was right, to a certain extent, for some of the former Nor'westers aboard had not entirely forgotten the old Company.

They finally arrived at the Columbia, and in May, 1811, the stockaded loghouse had been built, and named Astoria. The *Tonquin* sailed for Vancouver; the Astorians set to work establishing other trading posts, and keeping the Indians quiet with the sight of a bottle which Mr. McDougal informed them contained the Spirit of Small Pox; and one day in July David Thompson came floating into Astoria, down the river. He might be a rival now, but just the same there was a tremendous Nor'wester reunion at the riverside. Mr. Thompson looked around, and after a while he went up river again, saying nothing in particular. But the *Tonquin* did not return. A terrible thing had happened, they found out afterwards. Captain Thorn had offended the Indians, they had raided the ship, almost everyone had been killed. The next day the Indians had returned for the loot, and the only survivor aboard, a clerk named Lewis—himself mortally wounded—had crept below and touched off the powder magazine.

Months later, when Mr. Astor heard of it, he called it "a calamity, the length of which I could not foresee." But he went to the theatre that evening—he was always very fond of the theatre—and to a friend who seemed surprised he said, "What would you have me do? Would you have me stay at home and weep for what I cannot help?"

Fortitude in Distress—but other shipowners would perhaps have been less unemotional.

5

No detailed history of Astoria can be given in these pages; the growth of the establishment, the coming and going of supply ships, the perplexities which beset these men, alone on the further side of America —one must turn to Mr. Irving's *Astoria* for these matters. One can only glance, too, at the Overlanders, that courageous expedition which antedated the Mormons and the Forty-niners, and concerning which one hears so little.

Thirty-five hundred circuitous miles from St. Louis to Astoria in some eleven months; river and plain, canyons and mountain passes, deserters, and traitors, and Indians, heat and terrible cold, privations and hunger—"our cold and hungry hearts"— it is a record of incredible hardships under the leadership of a boundlessly devoted, utterly inexperienced man. Once, for nearly ten days, some of them marched with nothing to eat. They had already eaten their moccasins. In the midst of it all, in the December mountain snows, a baby was born to the half-breed Dorion's Sioux wife. In February, 1812, they were at Astoria, and the guns of the fort were booming while the *voyageurs* hugged one another and danced. Mr. Astor, when he finally heard, was "ready to fall upon my knees in a transport of gratitude."

That was in June, 1813—his first news from Astoria—but now there was war with England, and the Nor'westers were sending a ship escorted by British war vessels, to cooperate with an expedition down the Columbia for the purpose of seizing Astoria.

Mr. Astor begged the American Government to furnish aid, just forty or fifty soldiers, but the Government was busy. It did order a frigate, but the order was cancelled. "Our enterprise is grand," Mr. Astor wrote to his men, "and deserves success, and I hope in God it will meet it. If my object was merely gain of money, I should say think whether it is best to save what we can, and abandon the place; but the very idea is like a dagger to my heart."

And at Astoria they knew now that the Nor'westers were coming, and Duncan McDougal decided to evacuate ; but there were misunderstandings and dissensions, and the season passed. They must wait another year; and to keep the Indians friendly Mr. McDougal married chief Comcomly's daughter—a damsel adorned with fish oil and red clay who, according to Mr. Irving, was received "with devout, though decent joy by her expecting bridegroom," after she had been "freed from all adventitious tint and fragrance . . . by dint of copious ablutions." And in October, 1813, the Nor'westers were there—the land "brigades" under John McTavish—camped in front of the fort. Seventy-five arrogant, befringed and feathered Nor'westers against sixty, waiting for the British ships.

The young Astorians wanted to fight, and the Indians put on their war paint; the fort was well supplied, and a get-away up river could have perhaps been managed. It is easy, in retrospect, to demonstrate what might have been attempted, difficult to forget that Duncan McDougal was an old Nor'wester. He surrendered, accepting $40,000 for his stock of peltries worth more than $100,000. Perhaps he did it all for the best. When the British ships arrived in December, the American flag was hauled down. When the Astor supply ship arrived in the following February, Duncan McDougal was installed in the old Astoria fort as Chief Factor of the new North West Company post of Fort George. Many Astorians never forgave him.

"Had our place and our property been fairly captured," Mr. Astor complained later, "I should have preferred it; I should not feel as if I were disgraced."

As for the Nor'westers—they were to be smashed by the Hudson's Bay Company in 1821—"after their treatment of me I have no idea of remaining quiet and idle." He was still writing to Mr. Gallatin about it in 1835; and the old American Fur Company went on, filling Mr. Astor's coffers—and distributing smuggled whiskey to the Indians.

6

In spite of Astoria, it had been—it continued to be—very profitable, the fur and China trade, but Mr. Astor had another even better way of making money.

He had foreseen that the city of New York would grow, that what were farms and even waste lands, sometimes half submerged river front lands, in his time, would be hotel and business blocks in his children's day, if not indeed in his own.

And so he had been buying real estate, steadily buying, always on the advancing edges of the town; buying for very little, selling soon for more, buying again further along. Most astute transactions, some of them; such as his purchase for £20,000 of the English heirs' rights to the Morris estate, confiscated during the Revolution by the State—only the State had overlooked the fact that Colonel Morris had only a *life* interest in the estate. But Mr. Astor never overlooked such profitable legal details, and in the end, after a lawsuit in which the oratory of Mr. Webster and Mr. Van Buren was heard in vain, the State was obliged to compromise for some $500,000.

And Mr. Astor had a passion for farms—heavily mortgaged farms—such as the Cosine farm, and the Eden farm, a tract of land now known, in part, as Times Square. He was always buying up mortgages, or acquiring them through loans, and then as a rule he foreclosed them and purchased the property for ridiculous sums at the public sale. It was such a simple operation, this foreclosing of mortgages—especially during the trying days of 1812, and during the great panic of 1837 when he appeared as com-

ASTORIA

plainant in some sixty proceedings—and if it served to render him infinitely unpopular, it also served to establish the greatest fortune based on real estate in the country.

So great a fortune that in future generations it was to furnish the material for fantastic legends concerning its origin. The famous story, for instance—still occasionally current in the newspapers—according to which the Astor Estate is being sued for restitution, with accumulated interest, of the value of a trunkful of jewels stolen, at Mr. Astor's behest, from an island in Maine—a part of Captain Kidd's treasure, there buried. A most circumstantial and documented story, and utterly imaginary; the result of a magnificent hoax perpetrated for the amusement of the owners of the island by a literary friend. And among the papers of another old family there is supposed to exist the evidence of Mr. Astor's connection with a syndicate which was negotiating with the French Government, behind Mr. Jefferson's back, for the private purchase of Louisiana.

But Mr. Astor had no need of stolen jewels, and secret syndicates. The foreclosed mortgages were quite sufficient.

7

He died on March 29, 1848. "Bowed down with bodily infirmity for a long time," Mr. Hone recorded, "he has gone at last, and left reluctantly his unbounded wealth."

He had enjoyed his glass of beer, his pipe, a game of draughts, a little music, some horseback riding, and the theatre. He liked to have important people to dinner and literary men around him, and he befriended Mr. Irving and Mr. Halleck; in his later years he pensioned a friend to live with him, and speak German to him, and be "his trainbearer and prime minister," according to Mr. Hone. Aside from his wife's death, in 1834, he experienced one great sorrow in the person of "my unfortunate son," his oldest boy who was mentally deficient. At the end of his life he suffered from stomach trouble, he is said to have been tossed gently in a blanket as his only means of exercise, he had, literally, to be fed like a baby, and he fell into doddering senility. He was always kind and generous to his relatives. Almost his last public act was to foreclose a mortgage.

He left a fortune of twenty millions, eighteen of which he gave to his son William. To his native Waldorf he donated $50,000, to various benevolent institutions some $70,000, and to the City of New York, for a library, $400,000. There were no bequests to his servants and employees.

Many of his fellow citizens no doubt agreed with the New York *Herald* when it remarked that "the first idea we should have put into [Mr. Astor's] head would have been that one-half of his immense property—ten millions at least—belonged to the people of the city of New York. During the last fifty years . . . his property has been augmented . . . in value by the aggregate intelligence, industry, enterprise and commerce of New York fully to the amount of one-half its value. . . . Of course it is as plain as that two and two make four that the half of his immense estate . . . has accrued to him by the industry of the community. . . .

"We would have counselled John Jacob Astor to leave at least the half of his property for the benefit of the city of New York . . . leaving ten millions to be given to his relatives. . . . But instead of this he has only left less than half a million for a public library. . . . He has exhibited, at best, but the ingenious powers of a self-invented money making machine . . . without turning it to any permanent benefit to that community from whose industry he obtained half the amount of his fortune."

The butcher, the baker, the fortune maker.

Jay Cooke
The Tycoon

JAY COOKE

THE TYCOON

1

MIDAS, they were to call him, and the Napoleon of Finance, and the Tycoon.

He was born on August 10, 1821, "probably the first or nearly the first boy baby born in Sandusky," the third child of Eleutheros Cooke, a prosperous lawyer and Congressman, and Martha Caswell. He was named Jay for the Chief Justice.

It was a cheerful, well bred, hospitable home; always open to gatherings of friends come to partake of toast and oysters, as well as to the Indian chiefs who frequently visited the village, and especially at festival time when, as Jay remembered later, "the squaws were decorated with high plug hats, gay ribbons and beads . . . whilst the warriors were loaded with fire water, pipes and tobacco." And it was a happy, simple, open air boyhood in the Firelands of Ohio; a typical American rural boyhood. The horse to be watered and the firewood to be chopped; the village school and the private academy; candy pulls, and rat hunts, and the Philo Literati Debating Society; swimming holes, and little models of boats, and fishing and hunting rambles, sociables, and pigtailed girls, and a good boys' fight or two. New mown hay, and ginger cookies, and sleigh bells. And at home, a fine library, history, science, poetry, romance and "moral volumes on all subjects."

He was to have gone to Kenyon College; "you will see me digging up Kenyon hill of science next spring if God be willing," he wrote, in 1833, to his brother Pitt who was already there "under the discipline of instruction . . . toiling up the hill of science struggling to snatch the deathless laurels from the mountain's brow"—they must have talked like that in the Philo Literati Debating Society. But he had already, at the age of nine, helped in his uncle's store, and earned his spending money. "In fact, I was quite a capitalist"—he did not suspect how great a one—and in 1835 he accepted a clerkship in a large new store, under a proprietor who taught him chess and double entry book keeping. In 1836 there was an opening in the Seymour and Bool store in St. Louis, and he went there.

2

"Pitt, I have fine times," he wrote his brother, and his letters were always delightful, filled with news and politics, youthful philosophy and fun.

"Picture to yourself your brother Jay in a spacious ball room with a beautiful French brunette by his side, skipping along . . . and dressed in a fine brown coat . . . with white silk vest, black cassimere pants, white silk stockings, fine pumps . . . hair dressed and all erect talking Parley Voo with the beautiful creatures. Oh, don't mention it! Fine oysters here, Pitt. . . ."

Everything was "fine." He was going to writing and dancing school, and learning to speak French; there were fine hunting expeditions on the prairies, and a fine gaiety of fiddles in the old French mansions; although "there is but few respectable persons in St. Louis. It is dangerous for a person to go out after dark, for persons are often knocked down at the corners of the streets and robbed and frequently killed." But the panic of 1837 put an end to it all. The firm collapsed—Jay Cooke's first association with failure—and he went back to Sandusky, saying that he had "acquired southern habits and was a capitalist." The word was frequently on his tongue.

Back to Adams's Academy, in fact, but not for long. His brother-in-law, William Moorhead—who was always interesting himself in railroads and canals—had just established the Washington Packet Line between Philadelphia and Pittsburgh, and sent for Jay to come to the Philadelphia office. He was to book passengers, insert press notices and drum up trade at the steamboat landing in the face of an extremely stentorian and occasionally two fisted competition.

Jay did not like it at all. The work was hard and disagreeable, and "this great city . . . has no charms for me like those of my native home, and the deep, silent woods, and murmuring streams, and blue bay." He was homesick and he hated the "close, hot office," and the noisy town in which "fires and murders, mobs and abolition squabbles are every day occurrences." He was not sorry when the packet line failed; for a while he worked at the Congress Hall Hotel, but he disliked "counter jumping" and "polite and genteel employments"; Mr. Moorhead had finally been able to pay him something; and in November, 1838, he returned to Sandusky with "a trunk full of presents and plenty of cash in my pockets," feeling "as healthy as a rat in a granary," and planning to start a farm with his brother—this country boy who was one day to start a railroad across a continent.

3

But he was not to stay in Sandusky. Two gentlemen had noticed him at the Congress Hall Hotel, had been attracted to the tall, slender, light haired boy with the blue eyes and the cheerful smile which contemporaries spoke of as "radiant." They sent for him to give him a place in their office—Enoch

Clark and Edward Dodge, founders of the banking house of E. W. Clark and Company. He was not quite eighteen.

Brokerage and banking, it was the work for which he had been born. If ever a person was expressly put into the world to handle money—the actual currency and the far reaching negotiations arising from it—it was Jay Cooke. In a few weeks only, "I have got on the right side of fortune in Philadelphia," and "I am getting to be a good judge of bank-notes" —all the wretched, "shin plaster," "wild cat" notes of that hopelessly confused, pestiferous Jacksonian state banking era—"can tell counterfeits at sight, and know all or nearly all the broken banks in [America]." In the office, they called him "the counterfeit clerk," and marvelled to see with what "lightning rapidity the notes passed through his delicate fingers." There were no mistakes, no recounts; clean and dirty, "wild cat" and "par," it was all "easily and gracefully done."

They kept him busy, thirteen hours a day often. "It was a grand time for brokers and private banking." The partners, he found, "have frequently . . . gone off to dinner after overdrawing the bank account $80,000 or $100,000, leaving me to make it up before three o'clock." But "my bosses are making money fast"; the firm was a leader in railroad organization; during the Mexican War it was to be the foremost domestic exchange house in the country, and share with Corcoran and Riggs of Washington the task of financing the campaign; for young Jay, so capable and so trusted, it was a period of invaluable experience.

And his employers were "generous and noble men"; Philadelphia was now "really delightful," theatres, museums, dancing, some practicing on his flute and a little "gallanting"; he was devoted to his work, and "the same jolly, happy boy I always expect to be"; and he was learning to make money himself. But "I look upon riches but as naught more than the means whereby one can display his social and generous spirit, and, if I should ere be the one I may be, I'll be a friend, a man." A splendid boy of nineteen. Two years later, before he was twenty-two, they made him a partner; in the Philadelphia house first, and then in the St. Louis and New York branches. In the midst of it all, in 1844, he was married; to Dorothea Elizabeth Allen, of Baltimore and Lexington, Kentucky. "Libbie."

So it went, until the panic of 1857. "Money is not tight, it is not to be had at all. No money, no confidence and no value to anything." Mr. Cooke had already thought of retiring after Mr. Clark Senior's death in 1856, but he was still there when the crash came—the third failure in his career—all the Clark houses except the parent firm.

"Fight the battle out bravely," Mr. Cooke's father wrote to him, "and if all goes by the board come home . . . and I will give you a house and farm, and fowling piece and fishing apparatus, and wherewithal to live easier and happier than ever. . . . I have long regarded you as a gem, above all price . . . . I am ready to divide all I have with you at once. . . . You have earned a reputation for business capacity, for sterling integrity and noble benevolence of more value than millions of gold without it."

But all was not to go by the board. The firm was reorganized by Mr. Clark's sons; securities regained their value; and Mr. Cooke was able to retire, at last, with a "fair fortune." Again his thoughts turned towards Sandusky.

4

But his reputation as a promoting financier was too great; and while for a year or so he was "free foot" to hunt and fish, he was also engaged in "some vast and profitable enterprises"—the putting to rights of the Vermont Central Railroad, the reorganization of the Pennsylvania canal system, the rebuilding of the Franklin Railroad; and in January, 1861—at 114 South Third Street, next to the Girard bank—he opened the banking house of Jay Cooke and Company with William Moorhead, who was now President of the Philadelphia and Erie Railroad.

It was a precarious time to start a bank; the secession of South Carolina had already occurred, and there was war in the wind; but almost his first important transaction was the successful floating at par of the Pennsylvania State Loan of $3,000,000, in May; an undertaking the credit for which he shared with Drexel and Company, but the planning and execution of which were almost exclusively his own. "A glorious work" of national importance, demonstrating to other states that such loans could be sold "on patriotic principles more easily than on a basis of profit and loss," and "I am proud of it."

And for the next four years—aside from his ceaseless work in connection with lesser bond operations, and his continuous effort to maintain the value of government securities in the New York stock market, that playground of copperhead speculations and private gold corners—Mr. Cooke was to be known throughout the country for his astonishingly successful handling of the great Federal loans which financed the Civil War. What Mrs. Cooke, with her Southern relatives, thought of it is not recorded. For he won the war for the North, just as surely as the men in the field, and it was in the Treasury Department, a Confederate leader admitted, that the South was really defeated. The firm was new in 1861, it was not entangled in other affairs, he "felt it my duty to give a portion of my time and efforts to the work of raising funds for the use of the Treasury," and he instructed his brother Henry at Washington to tell his friend, Secretary Chase, "that I hold myself at his service and, pay or no pay"— he had already refused an appointment to the Mint— "I will do all I can to aid him in Treasury matters. I feel . . . that if he would give me a chance I could show him a way to raise money."

Something which Secretary Chase was at his solemn wits' ends to do. There can be no question, in these pages, of discussing the financial complexities of the Civil War—the acts of Congress, the banking laws, the intricacies of interest and maturity, of certificates, notes and coupon bonds, the "green-back" and legal tender debates, the frantic and sometimes apparently hopeless attempts on the part of the Treasury to meet the demands of an utterly unforeseen expenditure. These matters must be studied in Mr. Oberholtzer's *Jay Cooke, Financier of the Civil War*. But some understanding of the state of the Federal finances must be had in order to appreciate the magnitude, the vital significance to the Union cause, of Mr. Cooke's undertakings—undertakings similar, but on how different a scale, to those of Robert Morris during the Revolution.

And the Federal finances, in the early summer of 1861, were quite simply in the soup. The war was costing one million dollars a day; the public debt, when Secretary Chase took office in March, amounted to ninety millions; he had himself, in the course of a few months, been obliged to increase it by some twenty millions; in July, Congress was expecting to raise eighty millions in taxes, and was authorizing the Secretary to borrow two hundred and fifty millions more. Enormous sums which no one had envisaged, a small part only of the two thousand odd millions which were to be required. By the end of the year Mr. Chase had borrowed nearly two hundred millions, the expenditures for the fiscal year of 1861 had been more than five hundred millions, and the public debt called for another five hundred millions. Where was the necessary money to come from?

5

It came, the bulk of it, from what the Boston *Transcript* called the "greatest banking firm in the world. . . . Jay Cooke and the American people," by means of three great loans. It was Mr. Cooke who, immediately after Bull Run, personally raised two million dollars for the Government in a few hours. Mr. Cooke who accompanied Mr. Chase to New York, and persuaded the bankers of that reluctant metropolis to lend at once what they considered "the vast sum of $50,000,000" which they hoped would be "sufficient to end the war." Mr. Cooke who, in 1862, was appointed sole Fiscal Agent for the Government;

JAY COOKE
From a photograph by Gutekunst, Philadelphia
Reproduced in *The Chronicles of America*, Yale University Press

JAY COOKE

thereby exposing himself to the captious, niggardly moods of Mr. Chase's "somewhat precise and technical," politician's personality; to the unprofitable restrictions of inadequate expense accounts and commissions; to the continuous necessity of breaking the price of gold and buying up "every bond that offered below par," thus enhancing "the government credit at great risk" to himself; to endless banking jealousies and Congressional accusations of private enrichment; and to the vicious attacks of such helpful newspapers as the New York *Journal of Commerce,* the New York *Express,* and the New York *World.* And it was Mr. Cooke who, throughout the darkest days, sold the government bonds, took upon himself the responsibility of delivering them, and assumed the risks arising from the accumulation in his hands of every variety of currency received in payment.

One can only touch upon the conspicuous features of the three great loans. Of the first, $100,000,000 in 1861, Mr. Cooke disposed of perhaps one fourth of the total number of bonds sold by agents other than sub-treasuries—"seven-thirties," bonds bearing $7.30 interest. The second, in 1863—"five-twenties," bonds payable in not less than five nor more than twenty years—a loan of $500,000,000, was over subscribed by $11,000,000, Mr. Cooke's organization raising nearly $400,000,000. This was the bond which had been "repudiated by banks and bankers," but which Mr. Cooke so popularized that the Register of the Treasury could not sign them fast enough—$3,000,000 a day—until the delay in deliveries was become "ruinous." New Yorkers would have to admit, Mr. Moorhead wrote, "that our village can accomplish something as well as the great city of New York"; and "never before in the history of this or other countries has any financial emergency so vast in its proportions been so promptly met," Mr. Cooke notified his agents who sent word back to the Tycoon that "we congratulate *you* on the successful termination of the grandest financial triumph the world ever saw."

But Congress wanted to know all about the alleged efficiency, if not indeed the honesty, of "this rich banking firm which has been made rich by the drippings from the Treasury"—until Mr. Chase informed the inquisitors that the work could not have been performed "at all" by the Treasury, and that without Mr. Cooke "neither the army nor the navy, nor the general creditors of the Government could have been paid." And when all expenses and commissions to agents had been defrayed, Mr. Cooke found that he had cleared all of $220,000.

And then in 1865—after he had raised $5,000,000 in three days for a National Bank in hostile New York, and $7,000,000 more in the same place for the Government—Mr. Fessenden, the new Secretary of the Treasury, gave him the latest "seven-thirty" loan to handle. In one hundred and forty working days Mr. Cooke sold some $700,000,000. Nothing like it had ever been seen. The daily totals in May, his partners informed him, were "awful"—$140,000,000 in two weeks. And in the midst of it all Richmond had fallen and "all Washington was drunk"; and ten days later Mr. Lincoln had been assassinated and the Treasury had given Mr. Cooke *"carte blanche* to manage the market as you may deem best," in order that "government securities should stand like a rock." He went to New York, bought up $20,000,000 of bonds in a week, stopped the panic, and sold the bonds again at a profit to the Government "as I had directed an advance each day of $\frac{1}{8}$ on all the old issues of bonds."

He always "regarded this as among my greatest successes in finance," and kept the operation a secret for many years because "I preferred that the national credit should enjoy all the advantages of this action on my part."

6

The task of selling the loans was accomplished, primarily, in two ways—by means of the most far reaching personal solicitation, reinforced by the most widespread newspaper publicity. Mr. Cooke's agents —he employed some five thousand during the second "seven-thirty" drive—went everywhere; they overran the countrysides, visiting every last hamlet and farm, appealing to every living person they could find; they distributed posters and circulars—big broadsides, some of them, with eagles and mottoes on one side and popular songs on the back—in railroad stations, and courthouses, and hotels, in factories, in stores, in trains; they gave them to toll gate keepers, to post-masters, to the teamsters on the roads, they pasted them on walls, they put them up on trees, they tacked them on telegraph poles. And they interviewed newspaper editors.

From the very first, Mr. Cooke understood the value of newspaper publicity, the necessity of enlisting editorial cooperation. The people would buy the bonds if the newspapers told them to. And so he employed trained newspaper men on his own staff to handle his advertising; he filled the papers with optimistic notices, with "catechisms" answering all the questions which might occur to inexperienced investors, with articles praising the loans, the financial measures of the Government and the officials of the Treasury, with anecdotes of the prudent farmer, and the aged clergyman, and the timid widow with seven children—all of whom, including the children, had put their savings in government bonds. And he kept the reporters and editorial writers on his side, he entertained them, he made them presents of wine and game from his country place, he gave them options on blocks of bonds, he aroused them to patriotic support and, when necessary—as in the case of certain recalcitrant New York journals—he purchased their mercenary allegiance. It did not matter to Mr. Cooke, patriotism or cash—the papers must boom the loan.

Of course, at the back of it all, there was his own indefatigable industry; his cheerful, confident personality; his inexhaustible faith in the Union's credit, in the loyalty of its people and in the ultimate victory of its cause; his patient courtesy with hundreds of little subscribers who came daily to his office to be told about the loans, and it was "no small job to explain to so many ignorant people the whys and wherefores"; and above all, perhaps, the influence of his name which had become a national symbol of soundness and integrity. Jay Cooke—his loans, his bonds, his promise. The people trusted him. Seven hundred million dollars in one hundred and forty days.

And when it was all over, and the last loan was closed, they deluged him with letters, and telegrams, and editorials, telling him that the Rothschilds and the Barings were "curbstone brokers" compared to him, and that "the fame of Jay Cooke is now world wide." He was not quite forty-four, and his greatest undertaking, his most magnificent failure, were still before him.

7

"The Man Who Knew!" He was to answer to that toast at Tacoma, in 1891—in his seventieth year—at a banquet given to celebrate a task which he had begun, and which it had not been his privilege to finish. But he had known that it must be done, he had prepared the way and entreated success with courageous failure, he had always believed that the task would be performed.

In the midst of Mr. Cooke's official activities one is apt, perhaps, to forget that he was primarily, after 1860, a private broker and banker. The Philadelphia bank had prospered; a branch named Cooke Brothers and Company—in which Henry Cooke and Harris Fahnestock were partners—had been opened in Washington, in 1862; after the Civil War Mr. Cooke continued to interest himself in the national banks, in the maintenance of government bond values in the restive New York stock market, in the suppression of speculation—such as the Black Friday gold corner of 1869—and in the Treasury's various funding operations; and in March, 1866, he established his New York house. He was now the foremost financier in the country; his prestige was enormous, the reputation of his firm was unimpeachable, people came to him from all sides to solicit his financial interest. And those who came with railroads were the more readily welcome, for there was in his mind a vision of two oceans linked by rail, and so, in the late 1860s, he was willing to listen when some gentlemen spoke to him most earnestly of a road to be built across the continent and called the Northern Pacific.

It had been started in 1864, with a charter granted to a group of New England capitalists; but the enterprise had failed, the franchise had been purchased by the so called Vermont Clique, and now the directors wanted Mr. Cooke to sell the bonds. For a long time he hesitated, while his investigators travelled over the proposed ground and examined the resources of the section to be served; but their reports were all most favorable, grandiosely worded some of them, making of the Banana Belt—as the sceptics called it, from the resemblance of its contour to an elongated banana—a region of superlative climate, vegetation and opportunity; everyone was preparing to leave for Minnesota; and on January 1, 1870, Mr. Cooke accepted the Northern Pacific agency, and undertook the task of raising more than $100,-000,000—the great $5,600,000 "pool" first, with its special privileges, and then the bonds themselves, secured by public lands "to fall back upon at a fair cash price."

Lectures, inspection trips to the West for editors, newspaper ballyhoo—Mr. Cooke made use of all his publicity methods. The thing was a gamble, his partners were not in favor of the venture, railroads were a dubious speculation, but Mr. Cooke had set his heart and all his mind on putting through a road to the Pacific. It was more than just another "iron road"; there were branches and mergers involved, all manner of land and colonization schemes, the development of Duluth, the importation of laborers and settlers from abroad, the sale of securities in Europe and a labyrinth of Washington politics to be threaded. For any detailed account of these matters, of the internal extravagances and disputes, and of the furiously intricate financial arrangements, one must turn again to Mr. Oberholtzer's *Life of Jay Cooke*. They sold some bonds, they began to build, they completed some five hundred miles of line.

8

But under the surface things were not going at all well. The bonds were not selling, the company's funds were low, Mr. Cooke, with all his courage and optimism—some were to call it over-confidence and obstinacy—was carrying more than he could hold, than he had any right to attempt. His New York partner, Mr. Fahnestock, told him so very plainly, in June, 1872, in a letter which furnishes a very complete indictment of the Northern Pacific's status.

"No enterprise of such magnitude," he wrote, "has ever before been so entirely dependent upon one house, or rather upon one man," and it was "injudicious to make the reputation, if not the existence of a house . . . dependent upon the success or failure of an enterprise of unprecedented experiment." The firm, he reminded Mr. Cooke, and "especially you, are the Northern Pacific Railroad, and you have the additional delicate responsibility of the trusteeship, making you morally liable to every man and woman holding the bonds." Mr. Cooke had assured them of the "intelligence, vigor and economy of the management," and "we know that it has been inefficient, distracted by other engagements and extravagant to the last degree. . . . We know that a large proportion of the lands . . . are practically valueless . . . and that the residue are less valuable than the public have been led to believe"—a supposition in which Mr. Cooke did not concur.

At the same time, the bonds were being sold "almost exclusively to persons who rely upon our recommendations rather than upon their own judgments, and there is a limit to this class and their money." Enthusiasm alone was not sufficient. The sales were difficult and restricted because the bonds were useless as collateral, since "everybody knows that their value depends upon one man's ability to make them good." This was all wrong, and the enterprise was "at the mercy of any contingency which may arise to interrupt sales of bonds, stop the work and leave us to provide means to save the company from default. . . . Radical . . . changes are necessary to save the company from ingloriously breaking down within the next year and involving us in discredit, if not in ruin."

And conditions did not improve. The Franco-Prussian war had tightened money abroad, so that in Germany an American railroad bond would not sell "even if signed by an angel of Heaven"; at home, the company's subsidiary St. Paul and Pacific Railroad was in trouble and receiving no help from its parent, a circumstance which aroused popular suspicion concerning the latter's welfare as well; frequent gold speculations had disturbed the money market; at a time when Mr. Cooke was doing all in his power to raise funds through a syndicate, the public disgust over the Union Pacific scandals in Congress was turning investors away from railroads; interest payments were coming due to meet which the Cooke houses were obliged to make constant cash advances to the company, or see it collapse; "every day," Mr. Fahnestock had recently been writing, "we are getting in deeper . . . without any exaggeration we are in a perfectly helpless position."

But Mr. Cooke would not give in, he would not abandon the road, he would not desert this national enterprise. He was responsible to all those little investors. Jay Cooke—his road, his bonds, his prom-

JAY COOKE

ise. Something would turn up; there was no pressing emergency; September of 1873 came, and in New York money was "very firm, the stock market active and fluctuating, no immediate trouble apparently impending."

They were all, actually, dancing on the edge of a volcano.

9

On September 8, there was a failure in New York. Two days later the stock market was "excited"; it was "tremulous, uneasy and quickly affected by rumors"; there was a disposition "to create panic at the expense of reputation"; the names of respectable houses were being "bandied about" in connection with suspension and failure. On September 11, "a sense of calamity, indescribable and possibly superstitious, overhangs the Street." And on September 13, there was a "sensation." Kenyon, Cox and Company, of which Daniel Drew was a partner, had failed. "Who next?"

And a significant thing about these failures, the *Herald* pointed out, was that they were the result of—

"an effort to sustain railway projects which are apparently too weak to take care of themselves. It is a very nice question as to how many other similar schemes are being carried, and how much money has been loaned by banks on securities that have no immediate substance to them."

A very nice question which Mr. Fahnestock was also asking himself, no doubt, as he gazed at his useless Northern Pacific collateral.

And on the morning of September 18 there was "a financial hurricane in Wall Street," a "thunderbolt," as though the "bottom of Wall Street had literally dropped out." Jay Cooke and Company had closed its doors, to be followed almost at once by the Philadelphia and Washington houses. The Treasury's protégé, the Government's pet, the proud Tycoon had failed. In New York, Mr. Fahnestock had not even consulted Mr. Cooke. The great firm had "crashed," staggering under the burden of the Northern Pacific. At the New York Stock Exchange—

"a monstrous yell went up and seemed to ... shake the building. ... Stocks ... came tumbling down at a frightful rate and ... this only served to increase the hubbub to a demoniac revel. Many tore their hair and ran about as if crazy. ... The Stock Exchange had lost its head ... a stranger might have well believed himself in a mad house."

In front of the Cooke offices, at Nassau and Wall, an enormous mob was being kept back by "a cordon

JAY COOKE 75

of policemen looking gloomy but earnest." In Washington everyone was in the street, and a murder trial was immediately adjourned. At Philadelphia—where E. W. Clark and Company had also suspended—the Stock Board refused to believe the announcement of the failure, and a newsboy was arrested in the street for crying it. The pitiful crowds stayed all night, facing the closed doors.

There it was. Jay Cooke had failed, with assets double his liabilities. "No one who has a dollar on deposit here will lose it," Mr. Cooke insisted in Philadelphia. In New York, Mr. Fahnestock explained that "the immediate cause of the suspension . . . were the large drawings upon [his office] by their Philadelphia house and their own depositors. . . . The Philadelphia house had previously been weakened by large cash advances to the Northern Pacific." Yes, it was true, Mr. Fahnestock admitted, that he had been "taking the money placed in your bank by depositors to lend it to the Philadelphia house, which in turn loaned it to the Northern Pacific."

Commodore Vanderbilt was very solemn about it, very sage.

"People undertake to do about four times as much business as they can legitimately undertake," he complained. "There are a great many worthless railroads started . . . without any means to carry them through. Respectable banking houses . . . make themselves agents for the sale of the bonds. . . . Building railroads from nowhere to nowhere at public expense is not a legitimate undertaking." And the New York *Herald* was very stern. "This Northern Pacific Railroad was a stupendous speculation," it decided. "The Cookes were either shortsighted . . . or they calculated upon tempting the market and public . . . by extensive advertising and the prestige of their financial standing. . . .

"While giving the Cookes credit for ability, enterprise, liberality. . . we cannot excuse the reckless speculation and vaulting ambition that looks like gambling. They ought to have had more regard for public and great business interests, for they were trusted agents of the Government"—something which annoyed the *Herald*—"looked upon as the pillars and advocates of the national banking system, and claimed more than any other bankers the confidence of the people."

From other sources Mr. Cooke received only sympathy and respect.

"Not a single whisper of dishonor was heard against him or his house," the Philadelphia *Inquirer* proclaimed. "The house suspended because its chief essayed to assist . . . a work for the common good of the country and of humanity." And the New York *Tribune* found that "nothing can ob-

A TIGHT DAY AT THE DISCOUNT DESK
From a contemporary print

JAY COOKE

scure the fact that the very enterprise which has finally dragged [him] down was of national concern. Whatever may be the result . . . we shall regard the disaster to Jay Cooke and Company as nothing less than a public calamity."

Of course Mr. Cooke was obliged to read a great many personal letters from depositors such as the one reminding him that "you told me and my little girl . . . that all was safe, and if anything happened to the bank you would let us know. Did you do it?"

10

In spite of the *Herald's* conviction that the country was "too prosperous and wealthy to be seriously disturbed by the collapse of a few speculators or ephemeral banking institutions" dealing in "insecurities"—the crash of Jay Cooke precipitated the great panic of 1873. When he fell from the financial firmament whole universes fell with him. On September 19, in the pouring rain, Wall Street was "one mass of men" from Broadway to Hanover Street; the scene in the Stock Exchange was "one of those wild, frenzied exhibitions that periodically occur in that remarkable institution"; and on the following morning the Exchange was closed, with an "immense shout that . . . shook the roof . . . and a terrific rush for the doors." It did not reopen until September 30. On

September 21, fifty-six firms had already failed in New York, Philadelphia, Chicago and other cities.

At night the Fifth Avenue Hotel was jammed by "all the magnates in the commercial, financial and political world"; and there, on September 21, President Grant and Secretary of the Treasury Richardson refused—and quite properly for all its generosity—Commodore Vanderbilt's offer of $10,000,000 if the Government would lend another $30,000,000 to the banks; and decided, instead, on the measures which finally relieved the pressure and stopped the panic—clearing house loan certificates and a liberal purchase of government bonds by the Treasury. "Calm and order" returned to Wall Street and "hereafter the bulls and bears . . . may tear each other to pieces and they will only be regarded by solid business men as so many marionettes playing their puppet parts." So it seemed to the omniscient *Herald*.

And in Philadelphia the creditors insisted on involuntary bankruptcy; a receiver was appointed, and finally a trustee with a committee of five; and the liquidation of Jay Cooke and Company ran its course. Mr. Cooke sold his estates—"Gibraltar" on Lake Erie and the country place at Ogontz, the wonderful show place which he had built in 1865—and retired to a small cottage. He was fifty-two, his business career was closed, poverty and disgrace had come upon his declining years, he had "gone up in the tower and looked around, and it will not be necessary to do so again." He was a failure.

11

But not at all. He was to live to see his road completed, after a period of bankruptcy of its own, and Duluth become the industrial center which he had foreseen; and he was to engage in one more business venture and find in it success and final rehabilitation.

For one day a friend told him of a mine in Utah, the Horn Silver Mine, the owners of which were in distress, and after a careful investigation Mr. Cooke took an interest in the property and set out to raise the capital needed to extend a railroad which must reach the mine. Half of it he raised in Utah, and for the other half he went to the last persons one would have expected, to his old speculating bugbear Jay Gould and his partner Sidney Dillon. Beggars must not be choosers. The Napoleon of Finance and the Wizard of Wall Street. "With us three men," Mr. Cooke remarked, "there is not the least occasion for a written agreement."

The road was finished, the mine prospered and paid Mr. Cooke $80,000 a year, in 1879 he sold out his share for one million dollars. In the space of five years he had lost one fortune and acquired another, more than adequate for his simple habits. It was his last financial transaction.

He bought back his properties of "Gibraltar" and "Ogontz"; but the latter was now too large for him, and all its furnishings were scattered, so he turned it over at a nominal price to the old Chestnut Street Seminary for Girls and built himself a new house not far away, near the village of Ogontz. There, busy with his farms, his vegetables, his butter and his eggs, and absorbed in a thousand kindly acts, he lived until his death on February 16, 1895, in his eighty-fourth year.

12

He was a courageous, far-seeing, patriotic financier, a magnetic and inspiring executive—only his own inspirations were not always shared by his associates—and a warm hearted, guileless, charitable man who bore no malice and did not understand deception.

He lived to give pleasure to others; riches, he had once said, were only the means "whereby one can display his social and generous spirit," and throughout his long life he never failed to cultivate his own. In the palmy days at "Ogontz" the place was always crowded with guests—five hundred at once at the house warming—and he was known everywhere for the excellence of his good cheer, the cordial unaffected quality of his hospitality which received the neighbor from next door as lavishly as the Presidents and Secretaries who so often claimed its bounty.

He did not care for race horses, and steam yachts, and fine clothes. He preferred a rough coat and cowhide boots, and the open country. "None of your derbies for me!" he once exclaimed. "You can't stick fish hooks in the brim." He was devoted to his Lake Erie island, he liked to play muggins, and above all he loved to hunt and fish—whenever he could get away, at his various lodges, and especially at "Gibraltar" where they often caught three hundred bass a day to be distributed all around the neighborhood.

And his charity was a constant, personal concern to him. Deeply religious—a benefactor of churches throughout the country and a Sunday School teacher who, whenever he travelled, carried with him gifts of Bibles and hymn books reinforced with fruit and candy—the favorite recipients of his thoughtful and discriminating benevolence were always the clergymen with whom he came in contact. And for those who could not afford a holiday from their parishes, "Gibraltar" was open every summer—two weeks at a time, all travelling expenses paid and no families allowed; a complete rest, and a long list of applicants always, eagerly awaiting their turn.

But the finest thing of all was "O. P. J." The

initials stood for Old Patriarch Jacob, and to him, during the entire course of the existence of Jay Cooke and Company, was given one-tenth of the annual profits of the firm before any division was made among the partners—a fund of many thousands of accumulating dollars from which, supplemented by his own private contributions, was financed the long list of Mr. Cooke's individual and frequently anonymous charities to needy persons in every walk of life.

"I'll be a friend, a man!" he had assured his brother when he was only nineteen, and in all his days, according to his means, he tried to keep that promise. An old gentleman, in his last years, with a long white beard, in a big cape and a wide brimmed grey felt hat. A patriarch himself, and much beloved.

Daniel Drew
The Old Man of the Street

DANIEL DREW

THE OLD MAN OF THE STREET

1

"DANIEL says up, Erie goes up. Daniel says down, Erie goes down. Daniel says wiggle-waggle, Erie bobs both ways." So, it is reported, they spoke of "Uncle" Daniel Drew in Wall Street, during the palmy days of his association with the Erie Railroad.

And with Daniel Drew one approaches perhaps the most fantastic era in American finance, to say nothing of legislative and judicial corruption; the era immediately following the Civil War, an era of predatory speculation in which, under a sky clouded with mercenary injunctions, several gentlemen in New York tried a number of things for the first time and found them astonishingly profitable. Daniel Drew, for one, the Mephistopheles of the Stock Exchange, the Fagin of Wall Street; and his two apprentices, Jay Gould and the incredible Jimmy Fisk, adepts who soon improved upon their old master's instruction. And their ally, the imperishable Mr. Tweed.

And in the background, with but not of them—and not so much with as against them—the great Cornelius Vanderbilt. Drew, Fisk, Gould, Vanderbilt—three Bears and a Bull—their careers are closely interlocked, and it is only through an examination of their common enterprises that one may attempt any discussion of their individual achievements. A complicated recital involving, necessarily, a certain neglect of actual chronology, an inevitable omission of many minor undertakings.

He was born in 1797, this Danny Drew, on a farm near Carmel, in Putnam County, New York, the son of respectable parents. He grew up a farmer's boy, tall, hardy and almost entirely illiterate, shrewd and sharp to his marrow, a cracker of rural jokes which he accompanied with the chuckling cackle which was his laughter. In 1814, he sold himself out for a hundred dollars as a draft substitute, and served for a few months in the State militia; at the peace he went home and trafficked illegally in "bob-veal"; and soon after that he joined a travelling circus, or rather a Menagerie, a "Great Moral Exhibition" in fact, since the circus was considered immoral. They were the rage just then, these rolling shows, and Putnam and Westchester Counties were their winterquarters where the talk was all of Hakaliah Bailey's new elephant and Howe and Crane's Great London Menagerie, and it was with Nate Howe that Danny became a driver and handy man, clown and ballyhoo artist.

But the circus was too immoral for him; Daniel got religion—he was to have recurring attacks of it—he left the circus and became a drover. A very prosperous drover who secured his cattle from the farmers on credit and then sometimes—so they said—forgot to come by that way again for quite a long while, and of whom Henry Astor and the other New York butchers at the Bull's Head Tavern told unkind stories regarding his habit of watering his stock just prior to a sale, having previously fed them salt in large quantities. But he was to do even better in the future at "watering stock." In the meantime he made money; he was married, in 1820, to Roxana Mead; and after a few years he took her to live at the Bull's Head Tavern which he had leased—the drovers' tavern on the Boston Post Road, so famous for its cellar, and its turkey shoots, and its games of crack-loo—where he did a little intelligent horse trading and acted as banker for the village, when he was not away on some of his long trips to Ohio, and Kentucky, and even Illinois, buying up droves which he brought East at considerable profit.

2

And in the early 1830s he began to interest himself in steamboats.

The great Fulton-Livingston monopoly, supported by the Legislature of New York, had been smashed in 1824; William Gibbons of New Jersey had put side wheels on his ferry *Bellona* and sent her back and forth on the New Brunswick–New York run— commanded by his young captain, Cornelius Vanderbuilt—thereby precipitating the famous suit as a result of which the laws of New York prohibiting outside vessels from navigating the waters of the State "by means of fire or steam" had been declared "repugnant to the Constitution and void" by the Supreme Court; Isaac Newton, Memnemon Sanford, Charles Morgan, "Live Oak" George Law—all the outsiders were at it, running steamboats up and down the Hudson.

And pretty soon, in 1829, Captain Vanderbilt was at it on his own, operating a route to Peekskill, in the boats of which Daniel Drew travelled when he went to visit his "Drewsclift" farm at Carmel. And perhaps because the two men were destined to get in each other's way for the next forty years in the most amicably ferocious competition, Mr. Drew put a thousand dollars in a rival company and tried to run the Captain's *Cinderella* off the river with his *Water Witch*. Instead of which she lost ten thousand dollars, and Mr. Drew had to raise more money from the Putnam county farmers in order to continue his rate war against the Vanderbilt "monopoly." But the

DANIEL DREW
From an engraving by Buttre

Cinderella held her own, and Mr. Drew quietly sold out to Captain Vanderbilt, to the intense annoyance of the other stockholders who had not been consulted.

Then there was the North River Association. Captain Vanderbilt pushed them so hard for a season that they bought him out. So Mr. Drew put on two boats against them and forced them to take him in to the directorate. Whereupon Mr. Drew put another boat on, in a dummy's name, and did so much harm to his own company that the other directors begged him to negotiate with the troublesome owner. Mr. Drew negotiated with himself for a while, and finally, on behalf of the dummy, accepted eight thousand dollars more than the directors had previously offered. Not long afterwards, making use in part of the funds out of which he had swindled them, Mr. Drew abandoned his partners, purchased several ships with which he raced the Association's crack *Swallow* to a frazzle, and then bought out the company and with Isaac Newton founded the famous People's Line.

For the next forty years Daniel Drew's name was to be associated with the river, connected with the splendid two and four-pipers of the Line—the *Rochester,* the *Knickerbocker,* the *Hendrick Hudson,* the *New World,* the *Drew,* the *Armenia* which went up and down the Hudson playing popular airs on a steam calliope. It was a bitter, reckless competition in the early days; a competition of cut-throat rate wars in which passengers were sometimes carried free; of captains who raced each other full blast past advertised stops—men like Commodore Hancox who thought nothing of firing rifle shots at opposing pilot houses when they pressed him too hard—and fouled competing boats in deliberately planned collisions; of tremendous flummery on the wharves where rival runners kidnapped passengers from other lines in a bedlam of vocal effort and pictorial flamboyancy. A baggage losing, ship straining, boiler bursting competition which took little heed of passengers' convenience or safety. So long as the money rolled in.

And Uncle Daniel was making money, and attending prayer meetings in Mulberry Street with increasing fervor, for religion had "got" him again.

3

At the same time, he was also attending to his little brokerage business; the firm of Drew, Robinson and Company which he had started, and which soon began to specialize in railroad and steamboat shares. Mr. Kelly the ex-drover, and Mr. Robinson the ex-circus man, and the Uncle who had known both employments.

And as the years passed and Mr. Drew became more and more prosperous—and built himself a fine brownstone house on Union Square with a shed behind for his black horse and his cow, and gave the money for a new church edifice for his congregation —it occurred to him that he would like to control the Erie Railroad. Mr. Vanderbilt, among others, was to have the same idea later, to control the Erie Railroad and make it pay, and that was Brother Drew's purpose—he was a Brother in his church—to make the Erie pay, with this difference, that Mr. Vanderbilt would probably have made it pay dividends to its stockholders whereas Mr. Drew only intended it to pay speculative profits to himself. And so he began by giving the New York Central lines preferential rates on his boats; then he obtained control of the steamers on Lake Erie which served the Erie; after that he bought the Buffalo and State Line Railroad; and when he had the Erie completely bottled up they made him a director.

But that was not enough. He must have the Erie in his satchel. Consequently when the directors decided to take the road into Jersey City and tunnel through Bergen Hill, Director Drew did all in his secret power to obstruct the undertaking without actually preventing it. There was trouble at Albany over the change in the charter, there were alarming rumors in Wall Street concerning the dangerous impracticability of the tunnel; Erie shares began to drop, its dividends commenced to dwindle, the road was obliged to borrow. "Deacon" Drew—he had so many names—stepped forward and loaned the money. In return he took a mortgage on the rolling stock. And they made him Treasurer.

And then the fun began, it had begun on the first day of his directorate in 1851, for Daniel Drew. He said "up," he said "down"—usually "down," for he was by instinct a Bear—he said "wiggle-waggle," and Erie stock obeyed. He began to make millions, and when they were not calling him The Big Bear they spoke of him as the Speculative Director. Of course, some of the money, within reason, should have been going into repairs and upkeep; the road had a bad name in those days for accidents, and one of its worst disasters occurred during Treasurer Drew's directorate; cars went over an embankment, and people were burned to death, and it was all because the rails were worn thin; but the Treasurer had been "wiggle-waggling" in the market and there was no money for rails. And in any case, he had been endowing a Ladies' Seminary and building several churches.

What he enjoyed most of all perhaps—aside from his revivalist prayer meetings and Sunday School classes, which took up several of his evenings a week now—was lending money to his railroad, because then they gave him shares and convertible bonds as collateral. In 1866, for instance. They needed $3,500,000, and as security they entrusted to him a block of unissued stock and some $3,000,000 of convertible bonds. Erie was selling around 95 in a rising market. Mr. Drew began to sell short; the market continued to rise; Erie shares were scarcer than hen's teeth; Mr. Drew became more and more gloomy. But when they thought that they had him cornered he turned to the Erie's $3,000,000 of convertible bonds, he appropriated them, he converted them, he dumped them on the market. Erie fell to 50, and Mr. Drew made several million dollars in an extremely original manner.

It was after a deal like that that he used to cackle, and earn for himself the name of The Merry Old Gentleman of Wall Street.

4

He made millions out of the Erie Railroad, using his position as Treasurer, and the funds and secret information which it made available to him, in order to manipulate its stock to his constant personal profit; just as during the Civil War he had fattened on the national distress. Not that he was alone in this. New York City was not at all times conspicuous for its patriotic support of the war; Mr. Cooke had infinite trouble in securing adequate financial cooperation within its boundaries for the Federal loans and bonds; many local bankers and brokers found it more lucrative to fish in the troubled public waters by means of a cold-blooded speculation emanating from the Stock Exchange and the Gold Room—a speculation reinforced by the bribery of telegraph, military and legislative officials, which welcomed the advance news of costly victories with "bullish" satisfaction and took advantage of disastrous emergencies to depress government securities, maintenance of the stability of which was a stringent necessity were the war successfully to be prosecuted. A speculation, on the part of the Bears, which croaked of defeat, foretold calamity and spread the rumors of panic when elsewhere, on scattered battlefields, with firm hope and confidence, other men were speculating with death. And Daniel Drew was always The Big Bear.

It is not an inspiring spectacle, the picture of this rapacious stock jobber, this unscrupulous trustee, this cackling, tobacco chewing old man approaching his seventies. And the picture is not improved, somehow, by the sight of him whining revivalist hymns at his prayer meetings, mouthing his sanctimonious homilies before gatherings of repentant sinners, preaching to children the doctrines of a faith which it was not in his treacherous, hypocritical nature to practice. A revolting old clown, speculating in salvation.

And they let him beguile them; they were glad to have him give his quarter of a million—or at least the income from it—for the Theological Seminary in New Jersey. The Drew Theological Seminary.

They opened it in November, 1867, just as the shameless Erie War was starting, and the Founder was there to inhale the incense of clerical praise and gratitude. "Oh, that we had one more Daniel Drew!" they exclaimed, for they did not "fear him . . . as a rich man," and "the church needs the money of its wealthy men." In fact, "nothing can be nobler than to give the funds and moneys which God himself has bestowed."

The speaker had better have said which Erie had bestowed.

5

One must pass over certain transactions the discussion of which fits more properly into other pages; the disastrous Harlem Railroad cornering contests with Commodore Vanderbilt, in the early 1860s; the struggle with the Commodore for the control of the Erie Railroad, in 1867, culminating in the sudden domination of its affairs by Jay Gould and the elimination of Daniel Drew from its directorate; the "lock up" of greenbacks with Mr. Gould and Mr. Fisk, in 1868, and the subsequent Erie corner which did not quite come off, even though Mr. Gould managed to milk Mr. Drew for half a million. In 1872, Mr. Drew had lost a good deal of money; he had broken with his old associate Jay Gould and was no longer on the "inside" of Erie; some of the newspapers were pillorying him unmercifully; down in the Street they were saying that he was done.

But not long afterwards he caught Mr. Gould heavily short of Erie, and made him dance to the tune that he had been playing to his Uncle Daniel a short while before; and in time Mr. Gould came to him, in his quiet, innocent little way, and proposed that bygones be bygones. Mr. Drew must join him in a little Erie "bull" movement which he was arranging. And not only that, but there was a "bear" operation under way in Northwestern which was certain to be most profitable. Uncle Daniel was only too eager to recoup some of his recent losses; his dividends were dwindling, creditors were pestering him, he was all entangled in lawsuits. He went out and bought all the Erie he could find, and sold Northwestern short in large quantities.

But unfortunately, as it turned out later, Mr. Gould was not arranging a little "bull" movement in Erie. On the contrary, he was selling it as fast as he could, in a rising market—to Mr. Drew's brokers. And as for Northwestern, what Mr. Gould had really planned for that stock was a "bull" pool. The more Mr. Drew sold short, the pleasanter the outlook became for Mr. Gould. On a certain day Northwestern hit 105, Mr. Gould had cornered the market, and the stock finally came to rest at 230. The Bears tried to have him arrested for some of his dealings in Erie, but in the end they had to settle, and Mr. Drew paid the piper to the tune of nearly a million dollars. This time they were right, Uncle Daniel was "done," and all New York laughed at the man who had been "one of the curses of the market for years past."

It was the beginning of final disaster. For almost immediately there was the panic of 1873; Kenyon, Cox and Company, of which he was a partner, went to the wall, and shared with Jay Cooke and Company the responsibility for the national crash which followed; another attempted gold corner brought Mr. Drew nothing but invective; a flyer in Wabash cost him another half million dollars; he was obliged to mortgage his house and put as much property as he could out of his own name; and in due time he was declared a bankrupt. The comedy was over. Except the comedy of avoiding his creditors and assuring them that he possessed only some five hundred dollars.

For a while he retired to Carmel, but the habit of Wall Street was too strong. He had to come back, and stay at the Hoffman House, and dabble in the market. But he was an outsider now, brokers would not trust him, they sold him out as soon as the market turned against him. Daniel Drew was over eighty, and he was done. They say he persuaded his son to come to New York and hire a house in

Forty-second Street, and put a stock ticker in the basement. He died there in 1879.

6

It is easy, of course, to misplace his actions in the general scheme of things, to forget the current state of mind in his pioneer days towards speculative enterprise, to lose sight of the fact that much of what he did was probably considered good business, shrewd, and smart, and legitimate, even when, as was often the case, his victims were chosen from among his own confiding friends and dependents. Especially if he went to church on Sundays, and frowned on theatre going and card playing. It was all new when he began—steamboats, and railroads, and big money—legal restrictions had not been developed, the idea of "service" had not yet freely entered into the conception of public transportation, the notion that the community or the state could possess any jurisdiction over privately owned public utilities was quite foreign to their proprietors' understanding. In many ways Daniel Drew was simply no better than his contemporaries, no worse than hundreds of respected associates during that dreadful shirt fronted, cigar reeking, graft beridden period of the Grant administrations. Indeed, with his absolute lack of refinement and education, his was a triumph of native

THE HUDSON RIVER STEAMER "DREW"
Courtesy of the Robert Fridenberg Galleries

wits and Yankee ingenuity. The cattle drover's, horse trader's agility of mind, which so appeals to the national imagination.

But in every community, no matter what the state of its business mentality, there exist certain fundamental instincts of honesty, of loyalty, of good faith. Somewhere, no matter how widespread and approved the contemporary corruption, men are to be found who, given the most ample opportunity, will not appropriate for their own use the funds entrusted to their care, will not gamble with the resources of corporations of which they are responsible officers, will not betray their partners and deliberately ruin their friends. There have always been such men; there were such men in 1870. It is the misfortune of Daniel Drew that he was not to be numbered among them.

Except for his People's Line—and some incongruous churches and seminaries—he left nothing behind him. His great rivals, Mr. Vanderbilt, Mr. Gould, even Mr. Fisk, all bequeathed something. They were, each in his own degree, violent and unscrupulous men of affairs, but they gave something to the nation. They were builders. Mr. Vanderbilt and Mr. Gould gave railroads, Mr. Fisk contributed largely to the gaiety of society. But Daniel Drew was a destroyer. He was a Bear, a pessimist, an opponent of prosperity, a decrier of the country's welfare, a profiteer in disaster. What he touched he damaged. He was an emptier of treasuries, a drainer of resources, a consumer of assets. Funds, credit, good name—there was always less of everything after Daniel Drew had passed by.

Cornelius Vanderbilt

The Commodore

CORNELIUS VANDERBILT

THE COMMODORE

1

"Law! What do I care about law? Hain't I got the power?" These robust and invigorating words —so typical of the ruthless, law unabiding business era in which they were pronounced—are reported to have been uttered during his later years by Cornelius Vanderbilt, or as he spelled it himself Van Derbilt —perhaps the greatest statute scorner of them all.

He was born on May 27, 1794, near Stapleton on Staten Island; the fourth of nine children of Cornelius Van Der Bilt, a Dutch farmer and ferryman, and his energetic wife Phebe Hand, herself a New Jersey farmer's daughter. "Young Cornele," a strong, big, healthy boy who worked on the farm and tended his father's boat; a great lover of horses who, at the age of six already, could race bareback against other boys; a lad who played hookey to go sailing, and swimming, and gallivanting across the countryside, and who sometimes talked of running away to sea.

But he was not yet to pass beyond the Narrows. On May 1, 1810, it was one hundred dollars that he wanted from his mother, to buy himself a harbor boat, a periagua, and become a boatman, and she promised him the money if he would plough and plant a certain rocky eight acre field by the twenty-seventh of the month, his sixteenth birthday. He persuaded the neighborhood boys to help him, and on the morning of his birthday he had the hundred dollars. Some seventy years later he had one hundred million.

It was slow work at first, for until he came of age he was obliged to give his parents the whole of his day and one half of his night earnings; but he worked so hard, he was such a good boatman, he was so frugal and steady, that in three years he made as many thousand dollars. And, while it interrupted commerce, the war of 1812 helped him at his trade, for the men-of-war in the Bay and the garrisons at the forts needed boat service all the time; and in the spring of 1814 he was given the contract for supplying the posts—one load a week to the three posts in the lower harbor and at Ward's Island, Harlem and Hurl Gate. Night work, all of it, and in the daytime he was at his regular Whitehall stand, one of the best known and most skillful young boatmen of the port. He slept on Sundays.

He made a great deal of money. He had already

in December, 1813, married Sophia Johnson; now, in 1814, he built the schooner *Dread,* and in 1815 the *Charlotte,* a trim, fast, coasting vessel in which he made several winter voyages to South Carolina. In 1818 he owned several boats and possessed nine thousand dollars. Young Cornele's position as a rising harbor boatman and owner of sailing vessels was established, so that people told him he was looney when he suddenly sold them all and accepted a position as a steamboat captain, at a salary of one thousand dollars a year. But Young Cornele knew what he was doing. With that extraordinary instinct which was one of his most conspicuous qualities, with that almost unnatural gift of prophecy, this young man had looked into the future, and on the rivers, and bays, and sounds of New York he had seen steamboats— just as fifty years or so later along their shores he was to see railroads.

2

His first command was the *Stoughtenger,* of the New York-New Brunswick ferry line owned by William Gibbons; a snorting little craft seventy-five feet long, which the natives derisively called the *Mouse-of-the-Mountain,* and propelled by inadequate "palmipedes" in order to get around the Fulton-Livingston monopoly on side wheels. For ten years Cornelius worked for Mr. Gibbons, living at the hotel in New Brunswick which they had leased to him rent free as a hopeless loss, and which Mrs. Vanderbilt turned into a clean, profitable hostelry. And if the *Mouse-of-the-Mountain* was a joke, the second boat, the *Bellona,* was well named, for they gave her side wheels and there was war, commercial war between New Jersey and New York arising from the legislatively authorized Fulton-Livingston steamboat monopoly in New York waters.

A business of injunctions, and seizures, and retaliatory laws, as a result of which Captain Vanderbilt was obliged frequently to leave his crew in New Jersey and bring his boat alone to her New York wharf, and then hide below from the process servers. Although when they caught him aboard he immediately cast off and threatened to carry the officer over to Jersey, to the jail which that State maintained for its New York monopolist enemies. And once they had him on the wharf, and took him triumphantly to Albany, only to find that he had purposely chartered his boat, for that day only, to a "monopoly" concern.

But in 1824, as has been related elsewhere in *Daniel Drew,* the great monopoly was smashed. The Gibbons ferry prospered and brought in $40,000 a year, but the Captain was beginning to think of other routes; and in 1828, when a newly enacted Jersey law angered Mr. Gibbons so that he withdrew his boats and offered him the *Bellona,* Captain Vanderbilt went into business for himself. He had the *Bellona;* in 1829 he built his first steamboat, the *Citizen,* more boats followed, and he was soon actively battling on the Hudson against other powerful owners who did their best to drive him off the river. But he was an energetic competitor; he loved nothing better than to war against "monopolies"; and these contests invariably ended in compromises favorable to him. In this manner he disposed of the Stevenses, of Daniel Drew on the Peekskill route, of the North River Association; before very long he was let alone to build and operate the fleet of some fifty boats which he controlled for more than thirty years upon the Hudson.

3

Fine boats, careering up and down the river in reckless competition with other lines, racing hammer and tongs with every rival four-piper. And not always successfully; as in 1845, when "Live Oak" George Law's *Oregon* ran the Vanderbilt *Traveller* to a dead heat; and in 1846, when, for a thousand dollar purse which aroused the partisan interest of the entire community, the *Oregon* beat the *Cornelius Vanderbilt.* Captain Vanderbilt was at the wheel himself, and lost several hundred yards at the turn by taking it at top speed, so that the *Oregon* came in ahead by some twelve hundred feet in sixty-six miles, burning bunks, furniture and partitions when her coal gave out. The Captain was very much miffed, nor did it soothe him to see Daniel Drew purchase the *Oregon* for his People's Line after her victory.

But the Vanderbilt boats made money; he was soon adding to his fleet and earning for himself his title of Commodore; and before very long he was operating in other waters. To the Connecticut River with his famous *Lexington*—the fastest boat of her day, commanded by the Commodore's brother, Jacob Vanderbilt of the later Staten Island ferries—against the Connecticut Steamboat Company; a vicious competition revealed in the company's notice proclaiming that their *Bunker Hill* would leave five minutes *after* the *Lexington* "to prevent the reckless destruction of their property and to protect their passengers from unnecessary dangers." And to Maine, against Memnemon Sanford's "monopolies." And with the *Lexington,* again, to Providence, to furnish the new railroad from Boston with a "through by daylight" service to New York.

And to Stonington, when the Boston railroad got down to it in 1837, to absorb the Stonington Line; an enterprise the stock of which kept passing through the Commodore's hands, and Daniel Drew's, and even James Fisk's, until well on in the 1860s. Another field for intense competition, for when the opposition *Richmond* began to beat all the company ships, the railroad offered Commodore Vanderbilt $60,000 for his celebrated *Lexington* if she could dispose of the *Richmond*. The *Lexington* was still commanded by Captain Jacob Vanderbilt, "whose reputation for reckless daring has been equalled by few and exceeded by none," and the Commodore had no misgivings concerning the outcome. The two boats started from Stonington, with the *Richmond* slightly in the lead, and for a dozen miles down the Sound there was no change in position. Then "dense clouds of smoke poured from *Lexington*, a sheet of flame shot up from her stack" and she began to gain on the *Richmond*. But now on the latter "a column of flame stood a pillar of fire above her. . . . The water seethed and boiled beneath her, fire and smoke were round about her overhead . . . she was a moving volcano." And the *Richmond* won by an hour.

It was the *Lexington's* last race, for in January, 1840, in one of the worst of the steamboat catastrophes—under another captain—she burned in the Sound, losing over a hundred lives, and "the lurid light of the blazing wreck shone far over the cold and dreary waste of waters."

4

The Commodore was taking in money through every porthole; he was in his fifties and had eleven children; and in 1854 he built himself the two thousand ton, two hundred and sixty foot long steam yacht *North Star,* and took his family with a chaplain and a doctor on a cruise to Europe. From Russia to Constantinople the *North Star* was a floating wonder, with her satinwood saloon furnished in rosewood upholstered with green plush velvet; her "elegant" staterooms, adorned with silk and lace in varying splendors of color; and her dining saloon of polished ligneous marble panelled with Naples granite, and medallions of Webster, Clay, Franklin and Washington on the ceiling, framed in a scrollwork of purple, green and gold. Nothing quite like it had ever been seen, not since Cleopatra's barge.

And when he came back to America, after firing salutes in honor of his aged mother in the little farm house on Staten Island—in the midst of another maritime enterprise to which one must shortly return—the Commodore, tired perhaps of river and sound boating, put himself in the transatlantic trade. It was like him to do that, all question of profits aside, to move forward always, to look ahead, to see beyond the horizon. While men like Daniel Drew were content with Albany and Stonington, the Commodore was sending ships to California and thinking of the Western Ocean.

And so, while the British Cunard ships were recovering from their enforced service to the Crimea, leav-

ing only the American Collins Line as a serious rival, Commodore Vanderbilt began to project a steamship line from New York to Southampton and Havre. The *North Star* was put on the run, and other fine ships were built, the *Ariel,* the *Ocean Queen,* the crack five thousand ton eight hundred thousand dollar *Vanderbilt* which he was to present as a gift to the Government during the Civil War—and receive for it a gold medal and "the thanks of Congress . . . for his unique manifestation of a fervid and large souled patriotism."

But Congress had already had an opportunity to speak of him, and in far less complimentary terms; for while the Commodore's earlier shipping activities had given occasion for an infinity of talk concerning the curious methods by which he was alleged to have influenced the disposal to him by the City of New York of dock and similar facilities, when it came to transatlantic traffic he found himself in the realm of Federal ship mail subsidies. And here one begins to have glimpses behind the scenes of the Commodore's positive business habits, of the enterprising means employed by him to increase his accumulating profits. For the whole matter of subsidies, recommended by the postal authorities, and culminating in the Congressional debates of 1858, was involved in a furious practice of bribery and lobbying in which the Commodore was not any less efficient than his competitors. And not only that, but the Commodore was accused of commercial intimidation.

Was it true, Representative Davis of Mississippi wanted to know—speaking of the Pacific Mail Company and its dealings with Commodore Vanderbilt, to which reference will again be made on a later page—that the company, which received a government subsidy, had been paying the Commodore $480,000 a year "in order to prevent all competition to their line"? And the Pacific Mail later testified that it was true; that for more than four years the greater part of their earnings "was wrongfully appropriated to Vanderbilt for blackmail," because "the terror of his name and capital would be effectual upon others who might be disposed to establish steamship lines." A state of affairs which induced Senator Toombs to exclaim that "you give $900,000 a year to carry the mails to California, and Vanderbilt compels the contractors to give him $56,000 a month to keep quiet." The Pacific Mail were plundering the Government, but "old Vanderbilt" was "the kingfish that is robbing the small plunderers."

So they talked in 1858, but the "kingfish" was not dismayed, he was never to be dismayed; and when the subsidy to the Collins Line was finally abolished, there was nothing for the *Ariel* and the *Vanderbilt* to do except to race the Collins liners off the ocean. For several years the Vanderbilt Line flourished, until the Civil War came to disrupt shipping affairs. The Civil War, and a change of vision which turned the Commodore entirely away from steamboats.

5

But the Western Ocean had not been the first blue water to attract his attention. In 1849, at the time of the Gold Rush, Commodore Vanderbilt—for whom monopolies were always a red rag unless he owned them—could see no reason why the new Pacific Mail Company should remain undisputed in its handling of the traffic which went pouring across the Isthmus of Panama. In his opinion, just as good a service could be provided across Nicaragua, by making use of the country's lake and waterways. In fact, he proposed that a canal be constructed and, in 1849, organized for that purpose the American Atlantic and Pacific Ship Canal Company; but in 1850 the idea of a canal was abandoned and a new charter was obtained from the Nicaraguan Government for the Accessory Transit Company which was to operate a "transit" route across the country connecting with two steamship lines.

The Commodore visited Nicaragua, inspected the San Juan River, selected San Juan del Norte—later Greytown—as one terminal and founded San Juan del Sur on the Pacific side for the other, provided regular lines of steamers on both oceans and sent down the necessary boats for the river and lake service. All to the great annoyance of Commodore George Law and his Pacific Mail friends. And when his engineers assured him that it would be impossible to take the *Director* up the river to the lake, the Commodore went down again to Nicaragua, put himself at the *Director's* wheel and warped her up the rapids, tying down the safety valve and jumping obstructions "to the great terror of the whole party." But they should have known that for Cornelius Vanderbilt obstructions did not exist.

In a few years, the Transit was in full operation, carrying some two thousand passengers a month in boats as far as Virgin Bay on the lake, and then covering the remaining twelve miles to the Pacific in white and blue carriages, twenty-five in a convoy, behind double pairs of mules jingling along a newly constructed macadam road. It was an executive and engineering feat to be proud of, smashing the Pacific Mail monopoly and shortening the San Francisco journey by five hundred miles with a reduction in fare of three hundred dollars; and in 1853 Commodore Vanderbilt resigned the presidency to Charles Morgan, preparatory to his holiday in Europe. When he returned, he found that Mr. Morgan had been speculating with the Transit's affairs in a manner injurious to his own interests and sent him a characteristic message.

"I won't sue you," he is reported to have told him, "for the law is too slow. I will ruin you."

And in February, 1856, he had ousted Mr. Morgan and was again president of the Transit Company. And in Nicaragua, a certain William Walker was now Dictator.

6

The Grey Eyed Man of Destiny. He was an American adventurer with already one California filibustering escapade behind him, who, in June, 1855 —at the invitation of the Liberalists in revolution ridden Nicaragua– landed at Realejo and in a few months, under the protection of the dummy President Rivas, made himself master of the country. His popularity in America was enormous; his *de facto* government was recognized at Washington; everywhere, in pro-slavery circles, he was looked upon as a crusader, an apostle of expansion whose mission it was to bring about the annexation of Nicaragua as a Southern territory—a conception of his ambitions quite foreign to his own private understanding of them.

And now the Nicaragua comedy, which was to be a melodrama, began. Twenty thousand dollars in gold, first, loaned to Mr. Walker by Charles McDonald, a representative of Cornelius Garrison the San Francisco Transit manager, acting with the knowledge of Mr. Morgan, at that time still president of the Transit in New York. Mr. Walker accepted, and during the winter of 1855 recruits from America came pouring into Nicaragua aboard the Transit steamers; "emmigrants" carried free, in defiance of the neutrality laws and of protesting District Attorneys in New York; for was not the Transit Company a Nicaraguan corporation—and Commodore Vanderbilt and the other stockholders all insisted on it, and laughed at the Federal Government. And then in December, 1855, the secret reason for all this friendly aid on the part of Mr. Morgan and Mr. Garrison became apparent to all those concerned except the Commodore; for it was proposed to Mr. Walker, on the plea—and incidentally a just one—that the Transit Company had never fulfilled all of its charter obligations to the Nicaraguan Government, that he annul the charter and grant its privileges, naturally, to Mr. Morgan and Mr. Garrison.

Mr. Morgan was head of the Transit; the company was rendering valuable assistance; Mr. Walker had to choose between certain considerations of fair play and his recruits. He chose the recruits. In February, 1856, the old charter was revoked and a new one issued in favor of Mr. Garrison and Mr. Morgan. What Mr. Walker could not have foreseen, and did not discover until it was too late, was that in that same month Mr. Morgan had suddenly ceased to be head of the Transit. Commodore Vanderbilt was again in control, and Mr. Walker had backed the wrong mule.

The Commodore was in a fine fury, and now it was the Federal Government's turn to laugh. The Transit Company was a Nicaraguan corporation, was it not? Very well then. Commodore Vanderbilt withdrew all his steamers, and for six weeks, until Mr. Morgan could set his own in motion, there was no service to Nicaragua. And when the Morgan boats did begin to run, almost every one of them carried Vanderbilt secret agents who went whispering in the ear of President Rivas, so that finally there was civil war in Nicaragua. And on top of it, during the summer of 1856, a coalition of four Central American republics against Mr. Walker which finally drove him into the city of Rivas.

Mr. Walker was in a fix, in spite of Commodore George Law who tried to send him ammunition, and Commodore Charles Morgan who was still sending him recruits, and Commodore Cornelius Vanderbilt who, at one time, would have been ready to compromise and send him money. The War of the Commodores they called it in New York.

7

And now came the melodrama; the personal vengeance of the greatest of the Commodores. For in

November, 1856, Sylvanus Spencer, an American, accompanied by the Englishman Webster approached President Mora of Costa Rica with a very pretty little plan. With a hundred Costa Ricans or so they would proceed secretly down the San Carlos River to its junction with the San Juan, seize San Juan del Norte on the one hand and the lake steamers on the other, and cut the Transit. Mr. Walker would be isolated from all further American aid, and his defeat at the hands of the coalition must follow inevitably. President Mora agreed, and the thing was done; most successfully under the courageous leadership of Sylvanus Spencer, secret agent of Cornelius Vanderbilt.

The Morgan ships found the northern terminal closed; recruits could not be moved inland and a fearful congestion brought its disease and suffering; the Morgan ships were withdrawn. In Rivas, Mr. Walker coolly awaited the end—in the unexpected form of an American war vessel under a flag of truce which took him off to Panama, in May, 1857. The affair dwindled off into farce. Mr. Walker came back and was immediately removed again; Commodore Vanderbilt and his agents found themselves wading through a tropical swamp of Costa Rican-Nicaraguan intrigues and concessions; a busy French gentlemen made himself very helpful for a while, until his Government repudiated him; the Pacific Mail at last agreed to pay Commodore Vanderbilt the monthly bribe to abandon his Transit which so annoyed Congress subsequently. The Transit was not reopened, to the great relief of the Nicaraguans who were a little weary of all these American men of destiny. Mr. Walker, who would persist in returning to Central America, was finally shot, and so was President Rivas. Another dictator ruled in Nicaragua.

8

And in America the Civil War was being fought; the Commodore's youngest son, George Washington Vanderbilt, was receiving those injuries of which he later died; and the Commodore himself was presenting the *Vanderbilt* to the nation and earning the thanks of Congress.

At the same time, as a result of the management of the supplying of ships for the Banks expedition to New Orleans, he was very nearly being given a vote of censure in the Senate for executive negligence. The commissions charged by his intermediaries were exorbitant, some of the ships selected were rotten and absolutely unsuited to deep sea service, and others were over-crowded and poorly equipped. "The whole transaction shows a chapter of fraud from beginning to end," Senator Grimes of Iowa asserted, as chairman of the investigating committee. It was another Civil War scandal. And while Senator Hale wished Commodore Vanderbilt's name removed from the resolution of censure, and was "willing to pass him by and let him go," Senator Grimes held him peculiarly responsible, since the Commodore was the only civilian who had known the real destination of the ships, and the nature of the work demanded of them. "I think," the Senator insisted, "that he of all the men connected with [the expedition] was the most censurable."

At all events, there were no thanks from Congress for the Commodore's last shipping venture.

And the *Nation* was to have something to say, also, about his maritime enterprises.

"Perhaps some of our readers," it remarked in 1869, "may have had the fortune to go to California, or to Europe in steamships of which Mr. Vanderbilt had the control. They know, then, with how much respect the travelling public ought to recollect him. The accommodations on board the vessels, the food that was served, the condition as to seaworthiness of the ships themselves, and the efficiency of the officers and crews, the way in which the traveller was cared for whenever, by act of Providence, one of the steamers was wrecked or delayed, will be fresh in the memory of everybody who, by seafaring, has ever contributed of his substance to increase Mr. Vanderbilt's store."

But now the Commodore was almost seventy; he was said to be worth $10,000,000, practically all of it invested in steamboats; he was in very poor health. His long career was nearly over, there was very little left for him to do. So they thought. Actually he was to be married again, to a Southern lady; the most important period of his career had not yet begun; he was to do things during the next twelve years which made people forget the previous forty and increased his fortune tenfold. For again he saw a vision, he anticipated a change and foretold an era; and in the flick of an eyelash he sold all his boats and began to look at railroads.

9

"I am a friend of the iron road," Commodore Vanderbilt told a reporter during the panic of 1873, "and like to see it stretching to every corner of the United States. [Railroads] help to develop our commerce and civilization, and ought to be encouraged." It was only when they were built "from nowhere to nowhere" that he disapproved of them.

He had not always felt that way. During his steamboat days he had scorned railroads, and in 1833 he had been terribly injured in a New Jersey train accident. But in the 1860s he understood suddenly that transportation in America must depend more and more upon the locomotive. The time had come. And after selling all his boats, when he came to examine these railroads with which the commerce and traffic of the future were bound up, he found a labyrinth of little disconnected roads, improvidently managed, all cutting each other's throats in a senseless competition which plunged them, so frequently, into disastrous bankruptcies and receiverships.

There was the Erie Railroad, for instance, fighting the New York Central tooth and nail; and the Central itself ending at Albany, depending for its access to New York on Daniel Drew's steamboats during the season, and at other times on two separate lines, the Hudson River Railroad and the Harlem. And these little dinkie roads were not paying dividends, their stock was so much waste paper. All this was unprofitable and unnecessary, to the Commodore's way of thinking—a far seeing, constructive, pioneer way. Railroads should run from one logical terminal to another, they should be operated as a unit in any given territory, consolidation must replace futile independence. In this way dividends would accumulate, and efficiency of management bring prosperity. So it seemed to him. There was only one way to find out. Buy the Hudson River and the Harlem lines, gain control of the New York Central, combine the three roads into one. And perhaps take in the Erie as well. This was the task which the Commodore set himself to accomplish, in approximately his seventieth year.

10

The first part of it was not so difficult. Harlem stock—and later Hudson River—was selling for the echo of a song. Commodore Vanderbilt went out and bought it. He was no mere stock jobber; he believed in the future; in the market he was almost always to be a Bull, cheerful, confident and enterprising. When he wanted something he bought it, including Common Councils and Legislatures. He could well afford to. The Street smiled; here was the old Commodore, the steamboat man, the old ferry captain, buying railroad stock, poor railroad stock. Men like Daniel Drew licked their lips. The Commodore paid no attention. "All you have to do," he used to say, "is to attend to your business and go ahead." He kept on buying, and when he had gained control of the Harlem he built himself a tunnel through the Murray hill down into Fourth Avenue. And in April, 1863, the Common Council of the City granted him permission to construct a street railway from his terminal down to the Battery. Harlem stock began to rise.

And then it seems that Mr. Drew and Mr. Tweed put their heads together, and soon there was a rumor that the street railway franchise was to be revoked. Mr. Drew and Mr. Tweed, and, alas, some of the City Fathers, began to sell Harlem short. The Commodore went right on buying. On June 25 the Board of Aldermen annulled the franchise. Harlem dropped and the Commodore had been done—but when the Bears tried to secure their stock for delivery they found that he had not been done at all, for he had cornered the market. He settled with them finally at 179, and several million dollars passed into his coffers. The Street stopped smiling.

And in 1864 it happened again. The Legislature at Albany was discussing the Commodore's franchise, and preparing to pass the bill, when it occurred to some of the legislators that there was money to be made by selling Harlem short and then defeating the measure. Mr. Drew had also had the same idea. But the Commodore kept on buying, and before Mr. Drew and his friends realized what they were doing they had oversold the stock by some twenty-seven thousand shares. It was a very sad day among the Bears in Wall Street. Commodore Vanderbilt put several more million dollars away, at 285 a share of Harlem, and is reported to have remarked that he had "busted the whole Legislature, and scores of the honorable members had to go home without paying their board bills." As for Mr. Drew, it cost him nearly one million dollars; a compromise arrived at with the Commodore—so they said—in exchange for certain suggestions whispered in Mr. Tweed's ear concerning the Vanderbilt franchises.

And perhaps on this occasion the Commodore recited his favorite maxim to Mr. Drew—"Don't you never buy anything you don't want, nor sell anything you hain't got!"

Not long afterwards Commodore Vanderbilt had the Hudson River stock manipulated up to 180; the Harlem was paying high dividends for the first time in years; the Hudson River was doubling its earnings. Whatever he touched turned to gold. With practically no experience of railroads, and with only his energy and good sense to guide him—and a certain majestic disregard of statutory hindrances—he was proving himself to be a successful operator of railroads. No one had any longer the slightest notion of smiling at him in his new capacity.

11

And now for the New York Central, which would insist on patronizing Mr. Drew's boats with traffic. Except in winter when the boats were not running. And in January, 1867, in the midst of a terrific blizzard, the Hudson River Railroad trains refused to cross the bridge into Albany, leaving the passengers to walk over, dragging their baggage as best they could. A transaction characteristic of the monumental contempt of the day for the public and its welfare. A splendid object lesson for that son of the Commodore who may or may not, in a later time, have exclaimed "The Public be damned!"

The connection with the Central was broken, freight from the West began to accumulate, quantities of cattle had to be cared for, shipments commenced to pass over the Erie, and Central stock fell some thirty points. And when the Legislature asked Commodore Vanderbilt about it, he replied that he did not know anything about it since he had been at home playing whist, that there was a law forbidding any trains from crossing the bridge—which was perfectly true, as the Central itself had had it passed to prevent competition, only no one had remembered it—and that in any case it was "none of your business."

In the meantime he was busily buying up the falling Central shares; in a short while he held more than one fourth of the Central's stock; and at the end of the year a majority of the stockholders came and put the road in his lap, asking him to do for it what he had done for Harlem and Hudson River. There followed a little adventure with the Erie and Daniel Drew—an account of which appears elsewhere—in which Mr. Drew, for once in his life, got the better of the Commodore only to see a new face, that of Jay Gould, at the head of his directors' table; and in 1869 the Hudson River and the Central were incorporated as the New York Central and Hudson River

CORNELIUS VANDERBILT 127

Railroad, with a capital of $90,000,000. A little later the Harlem was leased to the new consolidation, with a high dividend guaranteed on its stock which remained in Vanderbilt hands. The thing was done.

12

He was to acquire other roads during the few remaining years, the Canada Southern, the Michigan Central, the Lake Shore which he found $7,000,000 in debt and provided with dividends in two years. He took them bankrupt and made them pay. He did more, the New York *Tribune* thought, to restore confidence in railroad management than any other man. He "ripped up the old iron rails," Mr. Hendrick writes,

"and relaid them with steel, put down four tracks where formerly there had been two, replaced wooden bridges with steel, discarded the old locomotives for new and more powerful ones, built splendid new terminals, introduced economies in a hundred directions . . . and transformed railroads that had formerly been the playthings of Wall Street and that frequently could not meet their payrolls into exceedingly profitable, high dividend paying properties."

He did it, he caused it to be done, himself; he held himself answerable to no one, least of all the public and the minority stockholders; the railroads belonged to him, literally in most cases; he was the sole authority, he was the directorate, he was—in so many instances—the law, he was Dictator. The country gained by it, he and his stockholders profited.

How he did it is another matter. A matter of financial persuasion, of Legislatures mollified, and courts of justice subsidized, of intrigue and speculations in the pursuit of which he was simply the most conspicuous and terrifying exponent of his era—an era, Mr. Hendrick brands it, "of ruthlessness, of personal selfishness, of corruption, of disregard of private rights, of contempt for law and Legislatures, and yet of vast and beneficial achievement." An era during which Mr. Conkling observed of one of the Commodore's lawyers that he was "the man that Vanderbilt sends to Albany every winter to say 'haw' and 'gee' to his cattle up there"—those honorable legislators of the period. In all these matters —and his steamboat years cannot have been very different—the Commodore was proverbial, he was superlative, he was utterly without restraint or diffidence. There was no fraud, no scandal, only a stupendous autocratism. He was the autocrat of the directors' table. He piled up his millions, and the stockholders did not suffer. The public paid.

And the Commodore's most favorite method of extracting payment was by "watering" his stock, by

THE STEAM YACHT "NORTH STAR"
From a contemporary woodcut

flooding it one might say. He was always increasing the capitalization of his roads. He gained control of the Hudson River, and issued $7,000,000 of new stock, at least one half of which was "water." He absorbed the Central, and inflated its stock by $23,000,000, none of which possessed any real value. He consolidated the two roads, and again inflated the stock by $23,000,000. Very secret transactions, some of these, exemplifying his formula for business success which set forth that "I never tell what I am going to do till I have done it." He told no one except two other directors, for instance, about that first $23,000,000 inflation; a little midnight operation at a private house as a result of which he probably acquired some $12,000,000, to say nothing of the profits accruing from his personal speculations in the stock.

The public paid and the roads paid. In two senses; for it was sometimes difficult to raise the $7,000,000 due the stockholders in annual dividends called for by these inflations, and so, in addition to exorbitant freight rates, there had to be "economies"; rolling stock was neglected, repairs were postponed, wages of employees were cut down. But from the Central alone the Commodore himself accumulated not less than $25,000,000, on which for the next eight years he was to receive 8%. And when he died, on January 4, 1877, after building a church and spending one million dollars to found a university, he had a little more than $100,000,000, some $80,000,000 of which including 87% of the New York Central, he bequeathed to his son William.

There it was—the fruit of an intensely irrigated husbandry, the spoils of a gigantic energy. The price paid by the public for some excellent railroads.

13

He was a giant, in energy, in imagination and in execution, and in stature. A tremendous, powerful man, with a splendid fighting head, white whiskers and hair in his last years, pink cheeks and fiery black eyes. When he drove in the Park, after the days of Cato's, behind his famous trotters—for he always loved horses—people turned and looked at him. The old Commodore. They knew him to be harsh and unapproachable, opinionated and abrupt; an all night gambler at whist at Saratoga; a suspicious, secretive person who kept his private papers in his bedroom; a scorner of society in his unadorned mansion on Washington Square; and an unbelievably vain creature—a gentleman who talked of putting up a monument in Central Park which should be the tallest monument in America, to the joint glory of George Washington and Cornelius Vanderbilt; a gentleman who did put up a gigantic, fearsome bronze statue of himself in a fur coat on the façade of his St. John's

Park terminal, which, the *Nation* thought crowned "with monumental incongruousness one of the most vulgar looking of all staring brick buildings."

They knew him to be all this; they supposed him to be hale and robust, hard headed and practical in the conduct of his astonishingly successful business, reasonably genial and amenable in his domestic relations. They were surprised to discover that he had been none of these things.

Actually, at the time of his death, the doctors recorded that he had "scarce a sound organ in his body"; he was "a dyspeptic through life"; he was a victim of almost every known intestinal, heart, kidney, liver and stomach disorder; during the last six months of his life he could hardly stand up; he once told a physician that "if all the devils in hell were concentrated in me I could not have suffered any more." One is in the presence of a most distressing physical condition which must inevitably have influenced his personality, borne with a magnificent fortitude reinforced by every sort of quackery. For he believed in mesmerism, in clairvoyance and in charms; he was convinced that certain individuals could see the interior of the human system by means of miniatures and locks of hair; he had a retinue of female mediums, masseuses and "magnetic" practitioners; he was amazingly superstitious—with his salt cellars under the legs of the bed.

Nor did he confine this charlatanism to his physical ailments, but sought the aid of spiritualism in his financial transactions, so that one is startled to hear of him summoning forth the corpulent ghost of Jim Fisk to a conference on railroad stocks. At the same time his desperate concern in religion increased with the passing years; *Pilgrim's Progress* had always been his travelling companion; now there was the solemn matter of the rich man entering into Heaven, until one of his magnetic doctors told him flatly that he would always be better at managing railroads than at playing the harp. Still, he believed that "Providence is as square as a brick." But he did not think it necessary to give away all his worldly goods to the poor, for it was his greatest wish to keep his fortune intact and to found a Vanderbilt dynasty.

And in his home, with his family, this curiously combined gentleman was a tartar, domineering, tempestuous and insulting. And not only during his last painful illness, when he would throw hot water bottles at his doctors and bellow profanely that they were "old Grannies" and "stupid fools," but at all times of his life. He must not be contradicted, he must not be opposed, he must not be interfered with; he flew into rages and quarrelled one by one with most of his children except William. And the latter was often enough called a "good for nothing," a "beetlehead," and a "blatherskite." But in time the

Commodore found that there was "something in the boy after all," he took him from his little farm at New Dorp and made him his associate, and at last handed him the presidency of the precious Central road and the greater part of his fortune.

It was not a happy family; not a pleasant home, this mansion in which a sick, ungracious, eccentric old man was thinking of "that paper" which was his will. The document which worried him so, because the money must as far as possible remain intact, it must be handed down to a single heir. At the end of it all the millions were a problem, an irritation, an anxiety.

And then, while the newspaper reporters stormed the house, the old Commodore faced that stronger Dictator than even he could aspire to be.

Jay Gould
The Wizard of Wall Street

JAY GOULD

THE WIZARD OF WALL STREET

1

"THE most hated man in America"—he said that himself. That was when they were calling him The Corsair and The Skunk of Wall Street, and his office the Bureau Ananias. That "saturnine little man," concerning whom, in the opinion of the New York *Herald,* "whatever Providence it is watches over [him], it is certain that his strokes of good luck always come in when least expected and are to the great detriment of other people. . . . It's always other persons' ill winds that do Mr. Gould the most good." But the *Herald* was not quite fair; he frequently foretold the winds, and often commanded them.

He was born on May 27, 1836, the son of Mary More and John Burr Gould, a dairyman of Roxbury, Delaware County, New York. The boy's grandfather, Captain Abraham Gould, but formerly Gold until 1806, had been one of the first settlers of Delaware County; coming from Fairfield, Connecticut, where his father, Colonel Abraham Gold, had served with distinction in the Revolutionary War, himself descended from the Worshipful Major Nathan Gold, Assistant Governor, and the Honorable Nathan Gold, Deputy Governor and Chief Justice of the Supreme Court. They gave the child the name Jason, but by the time he had begun to reach out for the Golden Fleece he was already signing it Jay.

It was a trying, sickly boyhood, tending his father's twenty cows while he "went barefoot and got thistles in my feet," and experiencing the riot and violence of the current Anti-Rent War. And schooling was difficult; but he worked for a while in a blacksmith's shop and saved some money; he was able to attend the local Beechwood Seminary where he wrote a fine essay setting forth that "Honesty is the Best Policy"; and finally he managed to get to Hobart Academy. At the age of fifteen he left school; he worked in the country store from six o'clock in the morning until ten at night, and got up at three o'clock every day to study mathematics in order to become a surveyor. And soon he was given a post as assistant to an engineer who was mapping Ulster County, and who cheated him out of his pay, so that he was almost always hungry, and ragged, and forlorn, and obliged to make sundials for the farmers in exchange for a few dollars. A miserable time, during which he found his only comfort in revivalist religion and in an occasional "cry."

But "there wasn't any foolishness in Jason's survey books," his associates remembered. "Even at meal times he was always talking maps." And when he had mapped Delaware and Albany Counties for himself, he had quite a sum of money and pushed on up into Ohio and Michigan, and wrote a history of his home county in his spare time. "Look at Gould," they said, "isn't he a driver?" He was a very courageous, enterprising young man in his twenties—he had already been to New York to try and sell the patent mouse trap of anecdotal fame—and attracted the attention of Zadoc Pratt, a well known New York politician and agriculturalist, who was interested in tanneries.

2

And almost immediately the mists of suspicion which were always to darken Mr. Gould's business career began to gather. For after setting up the Gouldsboro tannery for his young protégé, Mr. Pratt was not easy in his mind. The tannery accounts were so confused; the returns seemed inadequate; Jay —it was said—was interested in a private bank in Stroudsburg; and Mr. Pratt was glad to sell out to his manager. The money came from Charles Leupp, a New York leather merchant, and before very long Mr. Leupp was not easy in *his* mind. The tannery accounts were so confused; the returns seemed inadequate; Jay—Mr. Leupp thought—was speculating too heavily in hides. And after the panic of 1857 these speculations frightened Mr. Leupp so that he went home one day and shot himself. And a good many years later, on a day known as Black Friday, an infuriated crowd stood under the windows of Mr. Gould's office in New York, howling "Who killed Leupp?" But at the time, after Mr. Leupp's death, there was trouble of another sort; for Mr. Lee, the partner, tried to seize the tannery and garrison it, but Mr. Gould gathered together several hundred men and stormed the place, and won the tannery war. And for a while he was in New York, "Jay Gould, Leather Merchant." In 1863, he was married, to Miss Helen Miller.

But along with the tannery there was a little brokerage business, and, like Daniel Drew's, it began to occupy itself with railroads—the miserable, little run down railroads of that decade. The Rutland and Washington Railroad, for instance, the mortgage bonds of which were selling at ten cents on the dollar. Mr. Gould bought it, made himself President and Manager, and worked the bonds up to par. And the Cleveland and Pittsburgh Railroad, the stock of which he purchased at 70 and manipulated to 120 before leasing the road to the Pennsylvania for a good profit. Mr. Gould seemed to have a knack for railroads and their stocks, and so did an acquaintance of his in the Street, a certain James Fisk whom the incomparable Mr. Drew employed as one of his confidential brokers. And Mr. Drew was Treasurer of the Erie, that overripe plum among railroads of the day, and in 1867 both Mr. Gould and Mr. Fisk were members of his directorate.

It was the beginning of many fantastic episodes for the Erie Railroad, the gathering around its directors' table of these three personages. Mr. Drew already possessed a certain acquaintance with the more interesting financial possibilities of his property; Mr. Fisk had his own large ideas concerning the uses of a treasury; Mr. Gould was sitting quietly, staring behind his black whiskers, considering the advantages, it may be, of Honesty as a Policy; over in his office, Cornelius Vanderbilt was preparing a little surprise for his old friend Danny. One is to examine into these matters on a later page; it seems preferable, in this place, to disregard two years of exact chronology and to consider an event in which Mr. Gould and Mr. Fisk were concerned, in which the entire financial world of New York was very grievously concerned, and which left its lasting stain, in the popular conception, upon the name of Jay Gould.

3

The Gold Conspiracy. It is not necessary, here, to rehearse the previous Civil War financial history of the country, resulting in the existence of a double, gold and paper, standard of values; but Representative Garfield pointed to the fundamental cause of the gold panic of 1869 when he remarked that "so long as we have two standards of value recognized by law, which may be made to vary in respect to each other by artificial means, so long will speculation in the price of gold offer temptations too great to be resisted." In fact, speculation in gold prices, to the detriment of government securities, had been a notorious practice during the war on the part of many New York Gold Room brokers who were then spoken of as "General Lee's left wing" in Wall Street. "The business people of this land must have stability," Jay Cooke kept saying, "or we will become a nation of gamblers. This fluctuation daily in gold . . . affects everything else." But the fluctuation continued; an insane gambling on the rise and fall of gold which produced its Bulls and Bears, and "shorts" and "movements" precisely as in the stock market.

And in April, 1869, Mr. Gould bought $7,000,000 of gold and put the price up from 130 to 140, with the intention of buying more until he had bought it all, and putting the price still higher. It was a most

From an engraving by Hall

JAY GOULD 143

patriotic and businesslike "bull" movement, according to Mr. Gould, and his associate Mr. Fisk. It was to benefit the Western farmers at the time of their crop shipments. A perfectly sound theory, on the face of it, that "an advance in the price of gold would stimulate the sale of Western products, increase the business of transportation over the railroads and aid us in the payment of liabilities abroad." Mr. Gould's idea, so he explained it to Secretary of the Treasury Boutwell, was to "let gold go to a price that we can export our surplus products to pay our foreign debts, and the moment we turn the balance of trade in our favor gold will decline from natural causes." And Mr. Fisk saw it more bluntly in terms of Erie. "The whole movement," he testified, "was based upon a desire on our part to employ our men and work our power getting surplus crops moved East, and receiving for ourselves that portion of the transportation properly belonging to our road." For the railroads were "prostrated," and "as the representative of the largest corporation on the American continent, I say to you that we are starving to death."

But the scheme was to corner all the gold in circulation and put its price at least to 145. The fact that in order to transact foreign business, and in order to pay their customs duties, merchants *must* have gold, had probably not escaped the private contemplation of the gold Bulls; nor were they unaware of the prevailing speculative habit of selling gold short, and of the possibility of a strong decline in stocks coincident with a stringency of money.

And to corner all the gold in circulation—there was only $15,000,000 of it—was not so difficult a task for speculators possessed of the resources available to such men as Jay Gould and Jim Fisk of Erie. The thing that interested Mr. Gould was the Treasury's forthcoming policy concerning the $90,000,000 which it held in reserve. What would the Treasury be doing in August and September, hoarding gold or releasing it? It was all important to know.

The old system of "secret sales" of gold by the Government had been forbidden. Now, at the beginning of each month, the Secretary of the Treasury announced the sales of gold and the purchase of bonds to be made during the month. And very soon "an attempt was made to induce me," Mr. Boutwell records, "to make an announcement for two or three months." But "it was no part of my policy to regulate affairs in Wall Street. . . . I refrained from any interference with those who were engaged either in forcing up or forcing down the price of gold." Mr. Boutwell would not talk, although Mr. Cooke thought that he "ought to have an announced policy . . . that gold shall not go above . . . 40 or 45. . . . The gamblers would have someone stationed over them and be told that if they dared to combine to run up the premium, the Government would use its whole power to prevent it."

But Mr. Boutwell would announce no policy in advance; and Mr. Gould, allowing his glance to rest upon the elderly figure of that eminently respectable retired politician, Abel Corbin, began to think of President Grant. For Mr. Corbin was the President's brother-in-law.

4

Mr. Grant was a very unsophisticated gentleman who never seemed to realize that when birds are seen together they are assumed to be of a feather. And so when he passed through New York on his way to and from Boston, in June, he was willing to have Mr. Corbin introduce Mr. Gould and Mr. Fisk to him, and to sit with Mrs. Grant in a box at the opera house, in the company of the two directors of Erie—in fact, Mr. Gould was now in control of Erie. And when he went aboard Mr. Fisk's Fall River steamboat to go to Newport, Mr. Gould and Mr. Fisk were there too, ready to have supper with him and various other gentlemen, and "intending," as Mr. Fisk afterwards explained, "to relieve [the President] from any idea of putting the price of gold down." But Mr. Grant would only say that the fictitious bubble of national prosperity "might as well be tapped in one way as another"—and this, Mr.

Gould observed, "struck across us like a wet blanket." The President was a "contractionist."

Mr. Fisk became "scary" of the scheme—he was never really in favor of it—but Mr. Gould would not give up. There was always Mr. Corbin, who—it is Mr. Boutwell speaking—"under the influence of various considerations which appear to have been personal and pecuniary to a very large extent, lent himself to the task of influencing the President." Mr. Corbin, it seemed, heartily supported Mr. Gould's crop theory, and "the previous purchase and carrying of two millions of United States bonds by Mr. Gould for Corbin's profit may have aided in his conversion"—in the words of the Congressional investigating committee from whose report one must frequently quote.

Mr. Corbin apparently became "closely and intimately connected" with Mr. Gould in the successful effort to bring about the appointment of a new Assistant Treasurer at New York; an imprudent gentleman subsequently removed from office, who accepted a private loan from Mr. Gould, and denied that the latter had bought and carried for him $1,500,-000 of gold—something which later, in his own case, Mr. Corbin could not deny, although it seemed that Mrs. Corbin was the beneficiary. Mr. Corbin arranged interviews at his house with the President for Mr. Gould, even if "the President engaged in these conversations with reluctance" and would never say anything about the Government's gold policy. Mr. Corbin was very certain of his influence with his brother-in-law. Mr. Corbin was ready to do all sorts of things.

But Mr. Gould was not satisfied. He was buying gold all the time, but Mr. Fisk would not join him, his brokers were turning against him, his associates had "deserted me like rats from a ship." The Bears were selling gold, and Mr. Gould "did not want to buy so much gold. . . . I had to buy or else to back down and show the white feather." Something must be done to smoke out the President or the Treasury. And so Mr. Corbin prepared an article headed "Grant's financial policy," in which it was declared to be the intention of the administration to advance the price of gold. In his own devious ways Mr. Gould managed to have parts of the article printed in the New York *Times,* and wrote to Mr. Boutwell about it. But the Secretary's reply was "brief and formal." This was at the end of August.

And then a curious thing occurred. Mr. Grant, passing through New York and writing from Mr. Corbin's house on September 2 to Mr. Boutwell at his summer place, suggested to him that it would not be wise to sell gold in large amounts while the crops were moving. And Mr. Boutwell telegraphed to the Assistant Secretary at Washington not to sell "so large an amount during September as he had done in preceding months." And whether Mr. Gould "obtained any knowledge of this letter and telegram the [Congressional] committee [was] unable to determine"; but Mr. Gould was at Mr. Corbin's house on September 2, and during the next two days "gold again commenced to rise rapidly." And on September 12 Mr. Grant again wrote to Mr. Boutwell, saying that "a desperate struggle is now taking place, and each party [in the current gold speculation] wants the Government to help him out. I write this letter to advise you of what I think you may expect, to put you on your guard. I think, from the lights before me, I would move on without change until the present struggle is over"—*no selling* in large amounts, then.

One has, at this point, to share Mr. Cooke's faith in Mr. Grant, when he wrote that there was a "wicked want of honesty in high places and in all political circles," but that "Grant is the power, the glorious honest man in their path." For, as the minority report of the investigating committee did not hesitate to point out, "unconsciously or consciously the President in his letters to Mr. Boutwell worked in unison with the conspirators." Moreover, the minority deplored the fact that the committee had refused to call on Mr. Grant in person to explain these curious matters, and certain other startling de-

JAY GOULD 149

tails of evidence alleging that his relatives had profited during these days from speculations in gold. Allegations which the minority did not believe, but which it would have liked to hear denied.

Mr. Grant had simply become converted to Mr. Gould's crop theory; of his own accord, no doubt, and not at all as the result of the flimflam which Mr. Corbin was putting forward under what the committee considered "that worst form of hypocrisy which puts on the guise of religion and patriotism." But Mr. Corbin was very positive that he had influenced the President and could continue to do so, and kept repeating it to Mr. Gould; and, whether he believed it or not, Mr. Gould began repeating it very earnestly to Mr. Fisk of whose financial assistance he stood in urgent need. And on September 17 Mr. Fisk consented to join the Ring.

5

If in all this the President was perhaps a little of a dupe—and forgetful of the disastrous greenback "lock up" engineered by Mr. Gould not quite a year before—and Mr. Corbin a sanctimonious old fraud, and Mr. Gould an unscrupulous manipulator, Mr. Fisk, no less unscrupulous and fraudulent, was the country cousin to whom the gold bricks were sold. He was only too pleased to hear it, and to profit by it, but they told him that Mr. and Mrs. Grant, General Horace Porter the President's secretary, and the Assistant Treasurer at New York were "corruptly interested in the movement"; that everyone in authority was with the Ring, "beginning with President Grant and ending with the doorkeepers in Congress"; that Mr. Boutwell had been forbidden to sell any gold; and that the whole matter was "all fixed up . . . and Corbin has got Grant fixed all right."

And when Mr. Fisk went and asked Mr. Corbin about it, "he talked very shy . . . at first but finally came right out and told me that Mrs. Grant had an interest . . . that [he] held for himself about two millions of gold, five hundred thousand of which was for Mrs. Grant, and five hundred thousand for Porter. . . . He talked freely and repeated 'I tell you it is all right.' . . . I made up my mind that Corbin had told me the truth." And he believed Mrs. Corbin when she assured him that "I know there will be no gold sold by the Government; I am quite positive there will be no gold sold, for this is a chance of a life time for us; you need not have any uneasiness whatever."

That Mr. Fisk should have believed any of this nonsense—for there was never any evidence produced to corroborate it, and nonsense it must remain—is perhaps extremely significant of his own instinctive dishonesty; and even he never quite believed it, never felt absolutely confident that the Treasury gold would not be sold. "I had a phantom ahead of me all the time," he testified, "that this real gold would come out" and overwhelm the "phantom gold" in which they were all speculating so dizzily.

But he joined the movement "and brought to its aid all the force of his magnetic and infectious enthusiasm"; and the conspiracy of Catiline, it seemed to the investigating committee, found "a fitting parallel in the power which Fisk carried into Wall Street, when, followed by the thugs of Erie and the debauchees of the Opera House, he swept into the Gold Room and defied both the Street and the Treasury." Brokers were enlisted, a "national gold account" was opened, Mr. Gould and Mr. Fisk were steadily pushing up the price of gold and accumulating millions in "calls," while—

"with the great revenues of the Erie Railway . . . at their command, and having converted the Tenth National Bank into a manufactory of certified cheques to be used as cash at their pleasure, they terrified all opponents by the gigantic power of their combination, and amazed and dazzled the dissolute gamblers of Wall Street by declaring that they had in league with them the chief officers of the national Government."

The thing was suddenly become enormously threatening. Mr. Gould had been the brains of it, the strategy and the cunning, but Jim Fisk gave it life, and force, and brutality.

6

And because Mr. Gould was the brains of the enterprise, and not by nature a gambler at all but a dealer in certainties, he was still not satisfied, still not impressed by the optimistic Mr. Corbin's assurances. And so he persuaded him to write to Mr. Grant again, "urging him not to interfere in the gold market by ordering or permitting sales from the Treasury." The letter, with an introduction to General Porter, was carried by messenger—Mr. Fisk's selection for a man "who is a quick traveller, says nothing, but passes right along"—and reached the President near Pittsburgh. He was out on the lawn with General Porter, and when the messenger arrived these two warriors were playing croquet. There was no answer; Mr. Grant destroyed his letter; the messenger telegraphed to Mr. Fisk "LETTERS DELIVERED ALL RIGHT." Mr. Fisk read the telegram and misconstrued the "ALL RIGHT." He went on buying gold.

But it was not "all right." For on the evening of Wednesday, September 22, Mrs. Corbin had a letter from Mrs. Grant—the famous destroyed letter signed "Sis," which Mr. Corbin had so much trouble testifying about, because he was "a little excited, very weak and very nervous. I am perfectly broken down and there is but a wreck left." And in the letter Mrs. Grant had told Mrs. Corbin that the President wanted Mr. Corbin to "disengage himself" immediately from the gold speculators in New York. And the minority on the investigating committee promptly remarked that if the President had said that, then he must have known that Mr. Corbin was speculating.

But at midnight on Wednesday, at Mr. Corbin's house, Mr. Gould was not worrying about that. There was the letter, and its contents were disastrous. Far from being influenced by Mr. Corbin the President was angry with him, and there was no telling now what the Treasury might do. They had a disagreeable, anxious interview, Mr. Gould and Mr. Corbin, during the course of which Mr. Gould may or may not have offered Mr. Corbin $100,000 if he would remain in the pool. But it seems clear that Mr. Corbin did insist on closing out his gold transaction and receiving $100,000 in accrued profits, for the cheque, while never delivered, was signed the next morning.

And then Mr. Gould went home, after reminding Mr. Corbin that if the letter were made public "I am a ruined man." So, of course, would Mr. Fisk be a ruined man, Mr. Fisk and a great many brokers. But Mr. Fisk had not been told about the letter. There were only three people that Wednesday night in New

York who knew about the letter, Mr. and Mrs. Corbin, and Mr. Gould. And on Thursday morning Mr. Gould went to the Erie offices and said good day to Mr. Fisk, but still he did not tell him about the letter. For the little, silent man had thought of a way to save himself from ruin. While Mr. Fisk and the others were buying gold, Mr. Gould was going to *sell*. Secretly and deceptively, while pretending to be a Bull. An excellent idea.

7

Wall Street had already been "frantic" for some time, and the "gamblers of the Stock Exchange" holding such "high carnival" as had "rarely been known before." Mr. Boutwell, the New York *Tribune* was saying on that very Thursday morning, "appears to turn a deaf ear to the complaints of merchants who are groaning under the manipulations of the gold gamblers, and persists in keeping from eighty to one hundred millions in specie idle and useless in the Treasury vaults. This is very satisfactory and encouraging—to the gold speculators."

At all events, during the previous weeks, Mr. Gould had bought and loaned so much gold—Mr. Fisk's "phantom gold"—that he held "calls" on merchants and brokers for nearly $100,000,000. These enormous speculative purchases of gold had been made quite simply with the assistance of the Tenth

National Bank, "through the certification of cheques drawn by the brokers, and largely in excess of the balances due them upon the books of the bank when the certifications were made." A practice, this of "certifying cheques which do not represent cash deposits," which the investigating committee, busily locking stable doors, found "dangerous and pernicious." All over town, on Tuesday and Wednesday, merchants, bankers and brokers had been falling over themselves in a breathless attempt to secure gold and cover their contracts. And the more they tried, the higher the price went.

It is something to remember, in the midst of the uproar against the Bull ring, that there would never have been any Bull ring if there had not also been a great number of Bears selling gold "short," and speculating in that elusive commodity just as violently as Mr. Gould and his associates. Mr. Gould testified later that he had never originally intended that gold should go higher than 145, and that the panic which followed was due largely to frantic buying on the part of the "shorts." And Mr. Fisk was of the same opinion. "There is no fright," he said, "as great as the fright in Wall Street when the Bears get frightened." Gold went up "for the reason that there were in that market a hundred men short of gold. . . . They rushed into the market to cover their shorts. . . . There was a feeling that there was no gold in the market and that the Government would not let any gold go out."

Mr. Fisk did not discuss the extent to which he and Mr. Gould might have been responsible for the latter assumption.

8

And now it was Thursday, September 23. No one in Wall Street even suspected the existence of Mrs. Grant's letter to Mrs. Corbin. And Mr. Gould, who knew about it and realized on how flimsy a foundation the gold corner rested, did not tell anyone. His plans were made. While Mr. Fisk and his brokers were eagerly buying gold in the demented Gold Room, he was "quietly and rapidly selling as large amounts as possible without exciting the suspicions of his associates." He testified to it quite blandly afterwards. He had already been selling gold during the last weeks—he could not tell how much for "I carried the whole thing in my head. . . . I never kept a book in my life"—but on that Thursday "my purchases were very light. I was a seller of gold that day. I purchased merely enough to make believe that I was a Bull."

An amazingly courageous little "mouselike" man, really, sitting there at his trickery—for big Jim Fisk could have flattened him out with one hand at the first suspicion of his treachery.

But big Jim Fisk was over in the Gold Room in his shirt sleeves, offering to bet $50,000 that gold would hit 200, and laughing his head off at the terrified Bears. And gold closed at 144, with the clique in possession of "calls" amounting now to more than $100,000,000; which was $85,000,000 more than there was in actual circulation outside of the Sub-Treasury, so that "they seemed to be masters of the situation." So much so that during the evening they wondered if they could not publish a list of some two hundred and fifty well known firms which were "short" of gold, with the price at which they might settle. But that, it seemed, would be conspiracy, and nothing was further from Mr. Gould's mind than conspiracy—his conspiracy against Mr. Fisk always excepted. It was "one of Fisk's brilliant ideas," acquired from Daniel Drew, a certain broker related. "Fisk never could do anything regular. . . . He is an erratic sort of genius. I don't think anybody would want to follow him very long."

And so the idea was abandoned in favor of a more devil-catch-the-hindmost policy, and everyone went to bed, the Bulls and the Bears, the sheep and the goats. New York tried to sleep.

9

Early on Friday morning, September 24, the crowds began to thicken. Around the hotels, and saloons, and newspaper offices in front of the bulletins, and in the financial streets. Exchange Place, Broad, Wall and Nassau Streets were packed, New Street was "thronged, a tumultuous sea of excited men surged through it. . . . Business of nearly all kinds became suddenly stagnant and all classes and professions mingled . . . on the sidewalk." In and out through the tumult an enterprising peddler went crying his timely little gimcracks, a Bull and a Bear, and men incomprehensibly stopped long enough to smile and to buy them, guerdons of the forthcoming battle. Over at the offices of Heath and Company, Mr. Gould had slipped quietly into a back room; Mr. Fisk not at all quietly, having driven downtown in his barouche with two ladies of the theatre, as was his not infrequent custom; the whole place was patrolled by deputy sheriffs, policemen and "Erie thugs."

And in that room the final instructions were given to the brokers who were to conduct this "Bull Run of the stock campaign," this "utter rout, wreck and ruin of thousands," this "crisis of the first rank" precipitated in the midst of a "wild commotion" with which "nothing in the history of monetary affairs can compare." William Belden, a former partner of Mr. Fisk, in whose name all purchases of gold were ostensibly to be made—a very dangerous responsibility for Mr. Belden who, a few hours later, did not even know how much gold he had allowed to be bought in his own name, under Mr. Fisk's orders. William Smith, of Mr. Gould's firm of Smith, Gould and Martin. The pathetic Albert Speyers—or Speyer as some called him—a "deceived and confiding" gentleman who never suspected what was really going on, and who was to make a spectacle of himself in the Gold Room with his frenzied bidding and buying of $60,000,000.

But in one respect Mr. Speyers was not deceived. He understood what was behind Mr. Belden's name. For after the crash, when they tried to tell him that all his buying had been done for Mr. Belden and that he must look to him, Mr. Speyers retorted that it was "all nonsense to talk to me so. . . . Mr. Belden told me all the time that all those transactions were for one family . . . Smith, Gould and Martin, Mr. Fisk and several others." And in the Gold Room Mr. Speyers announced that he was buying for Mr. Gould and Mr. Fisk, and there were none at the time to contradict him. But that was the theory—Mr. Belden was purchasing gold for his own account, with Mr. Fisk in the background to give his orders financial standing in the eyes of selling brokers, and Mr. Speyers and the others were buying for Mr. Belden. They were to buy, buy all the time, buy all the gold that offered, at 145, at 150, at 200 if necessary. And for cash they relied on the complaisant Tenth National Bank and its "phantom" certified cheques.

And Mr. Gould—who was secretly selling, selling, selling, and making individual settlements with such merchants as contrived to fight their way into the building—Mr. Gould "had my own plans and did not mean that anybody should say that I had opened my mouth that day, and I did not." He just sat in a corner, and spoke no evil, saw none and heard none. Mr. Fisk, never a quiet person, was in the same room ordering the brokers around, but Mr. Gould heard nothing. "I did not pay any attention to what orders [Fisk] gave. . . . I sat in one corner of the room reading. . . . I did not want to seem to be listening to their business." Their business. In all that uproar the timid, retiring little man sat silently behind his mask of whiskers, watching his partners and associates go to probable destruction, knowing himself to be a traitor, a Bear in Bull's clothing. Nothing quite like it has ever been seen for cold-blooded nerve, for fishlike composure. He might still be looking for gold, the New York *Tribune* was to remark, "but no living mortal will hereafter suspect him of standing in need of brass."

Perhaps a little later he may have fallen to his trick of tearing off the corners of newspapers and crumpling them in his fingers. When the crowds outside began roaring "Who killed Leupp?" and "Lynch! Lynch!"

SCENE IN THE GOLD ROOM ON BLACK FRIDAY

From a woodcut in *Harper's Weekly*

10

The Stock Exchange opened, the crowds rolled in, "the curtain rose on an angry, furious scene." The Exchange was in a "condition of the wildest excitement, brokers driven half or wholly mad, and business completely suspended, all over the Union." Shares fell in an avalanche of panic, with Commodore Vanderbilt battling to hold up his stocks and advancing thousands of dollars to his associates who needed to make good their margins, "for," according to one broker, "the old rat never forgets his friends."

In the Gold Room, around the feeble little fountain, the "market opened tremulously. Anxiety and fear were upon every face . . . consternation and despair seized the Bears." The place was "crowded as it has never been crowded even in the wildest excitement of war times . . . aldermen and councilmen bespattered the marble floor with tobacco juice, deputy sheriffs without number leaned in convenient doorways." There was a "furious din," a "roar and tumult."

And then—one quotes largely from the New York *Nation*—

"amid the strangest variations of deathlike silence and tumultuous uproar, the pallid, half conscience-stricken brokers of [the] gambling clique appeared, one after another, to do their dirty work."

The bidding began. 145 for $100,000—no response. 146, 147, 148, 149 for $100,000, "with a pause between each, all amid deathlike silence." Then "the hundreds gathered there, and the thousands who read the ominous words on all the telegraph indicators . . . in the city"—some of them finally melted their wires, they were worked so rapidly—

"and the hundreds of thousands who watched the telegraph offices throughout the country, stood appalled. Each one per cent advance involved losses of millions. . . . And the usually surging, bustling, shouting mass of humanity crowded there was held silent, almost motionless."

150 for $100,000, and "the stillness is suddenly succeeded by frantic excitement." There was a rush to buy, telegraphic orders came pouring in, messenger boys from all over the city "force their way in through the crush." Pandemonium. "Transactions of enormous magnitude are made amid the wildest confusion and the most unearthly screaming of men . . . now driven to the verge of temporary insanity." They fought and yelled, cursed, and wept, and tore their hair, threatening to shoot the clique brokers, until Mr. Speyers got up on the platform and shouted "Well, shoot me. . . . I'm going to bid gold right up. . . . Here I am a good target! Shoot away!" Fortunes were being lost and won—

"publicly by hundreds of howling, desperate men, maddened out of all calculation by frightful alternations of hope and fear, protracted through fifty-six hours, and all this literally in the presence of an astonished, disgusted and alarmed nation."

But—

"amid all the noise and confusion the penetrating voices of the leading brokers of the clique are still heard advancing the price at each bid . . . until at last, with voice overtopping the Bedlam below, the memorable bid burst forth—160 *for any part of five millions.*"

A great silence clothed the room, "terror became depicted on every countenance," there was an "ashy paleness" on every face. "And from the silence again came forth that shrieking bid—160 for five millions."

It was Mr. Speyers—or Speyer—and, while he denied it subsequently, it was the opinion of most men present that he had for the time being become a "raving maniac." Mr. Fisk, who saw him soon after in the street, being dragged away, hatless and hysterical, by his friends, was of the opinion "that he was as crazy as a loon." And a gentleman in the New York *Tribune* who signed himself Edmund C. Stedman, said so in a long poem concerning "Israel Freyer."

"Up from the Gold Pit's nether hell,
While the innocent fountain rose and fell,
Loud and higher the bidding rose,
And the Bulls triumphant faced their foes.
It seemed as if Satan himself were in it,
Lifting it—one per cent a minute—
Through the bellowing broker, there amid,
Who made the terrible, final bid!
High over all and even higher
Was heard the voice of Israel Freyer—
A doleful knell in the storm swept mart—
'Five millions more, and for any part
I'll give One Hundred and Sixty!'"

11

The end came very suddenly, very dramatically. 160 for five millions. 161, 162 for five millions. 162 for any part of five millions. "And a quiet voice said 'Sold one million at 162.' The bid . . . was not renewed. But 161 was again bid for a million, and the same quiet voice said 'Sold,' and the bid . . . was not renewed. But 160 was again bid for five millions." Gold was going down. The quiet voice belonged to James Brown, a prominent merchant of the city. And to Mr. Brown, through his action in meeting the million dollar bids of the clique, belongs the honor of having defeated the Ring. For the news of Mr. Boutwell's telegram ordering the Sub-Treasury, with the President's approval, to sell $4,000,000 of gold did not reach the Gold Room until ten minutes after Mr. Brown's intrepid sales.

162, 161, 160 for five millions.

"Then dimly it dawned upon the quicker witted ones that . . . the game was up . . . A dozen men leapt furiously at the bidder and claimed to have sold the whole five millions. To their horror, the bidder stood his ground. . . . But before the words had fairly passed his lips, before the terror at his action had had time to gain men's hearts, there was a rush amid the crowd. New men, wild with fresh excitement, crowded to the barriers."

Mr. Boutwell's telegram had arrived, the Treasury was going to sell. In fifteen minutes gold fell from 160 to 133, and there were no buyers. None except Mr. Speyers who was still dementedly trying to offer 160 until his friends took him away. The "gigantic gold bubble had burst, and half of Wall Street was involved in ruin."

Including Mr. Belden, Mr. Speyers—who lost his seats on both the Stock Exchange and the Gold Board—Mr. Smith, Mr. Fisk and presumably Mr. Gould, of whom Mr. Fisk remarked that "there is nothing left of him but a heap of clothes and a pair of eyes." The panic had spread from Boston to San Francisco; in Philadelphia the indicator was draped in black and adorned with a death's head; much, in the imperishable words of Mr. Fisk, had "gone where the woodbine twineth," that is to say "up the spout."

The Ring, he thought, were "forty miles down the Delaware," and "it was each man drag out his own corpse."

12

And for a while it looked as though the mobs might drag out the corpses of Mr. Gould and Mr. Fisk. The offices of Smith, Gould and Martin, and of Heath and Company, where the "great Erie robbers" had sat watching the ruin they were causing "with devilish delight," were besieged by infuriated men clamoring to tear them limb from limb. But the buildings were swarming with deputy sheriffs, it was impossible to get in, and the "parcel of unscrupulous rogues" had decamped; Mr. Gould and Mr. Fisk in a hack with the blinds drawn, to their Castle Erie stronghold on Twenty-third Street. And what Mr. Fisk found to say to Mr. Gould during the drive one would give a great deal to know. For some reason he did not simply choke him to death.

For Mr. Fisk was boiling, and that evening—while the crowds at the Fifth Avenue Hotel were figuring hopefully that Mr. Gould had lost $30,000,000—Mr. Fisk "started right around to old Corbin's to rake him out." Mr. Corbin was—

"weeping and wailing," and Mr. Fisk was "gnashing my teeth"; and "Said I, 'you damned old scoundrel, do you know what has happened . . . do you know what you have done here, you and your people?' I knew that somebody had run a saw right into us, and said I, 'This whole damned thing has turned out just as I told you it would,' and I expected that when we came to clear our hands they would sock it right into us."

And when Mr. Corbin told him that he must be quiet, Mr. Fisk replied that—

"I didn't want to be quiet; I had no desire to ever be quiet again; and probably never should be quiet again. . . . He says, 'But my dear sir, you will lose your reason.' Says I, 'Speyers has already lost his reason; reason has gone out of everybody but me.'"

And then Mr. Corbin went to fetch his wife, and—

"they returned tottling into the room, looking older than Stephen Hopkins. His wife and he both looked like death. He was tottling just like that"—and Mr. Fisk "tottled" for the benefit of the Congressional investigating committee. And still Mrs. Corbin "thought Boutwell had [acted] in violation of the strict orders of the President not to sell gold."

Mr. Corbin thought so too, and offered to go to Washington to see the President; and Mr. Fisk "thought that the further off he was the happier I should be," and so Mr. and Mrs. Corbin departed on their wild goose chase to the chilly reticence of the

White House. And in his testimony concerning Mr. Gould and Mr. Fisk, Mr. Corbin was very positive that "there was not a word or thought of complaint against me by either of them; no series of words contained a word reflecting on me." Perhaps Mr. Corbin had expected so much that Mr. Fisk's observations appeared laudatory and sympathetic to him. For there can be no question of doubting the sincerity of Mr. Fisk's tumultuous recollections. "Said I, you damned old scoundrel!" His words to the committee came straight from a still bewildered and outraged heart.

13

$30,000,000 they were hoping that Mr. Gould had lost, but he had done no such thing. Smith, Gould and Martin did not fail; the Tenth National Bank did not close its doors; Mr. Gould himself, as a result of his prudent selling, came out some $11,000,000 to the good. What was the use! And Mr. Fisk did not lose much either, for in the morning all the purchases of gold made through Mr. Belden, a mere $70,000,000, were repudiated, and a dozen injunctions issued by the Erie judges forbade almost everybody to do anything. The Gold Room closed, the Gold Exchange bank went into the hands of a receiver, one panic after another swept the Stock Exchange. It was a long time before the tangle was unravelled.

"Plainly there is as little honor among gold gamblers," the New York *Tribune* complained, "as among thieves. They use lawyers' injunctions to prevent the payment of honest debts; obey the rules of the Gold Exchange when they make by it and repudiate when they lose; betray each other's counsels, sell out their confederates and consent to the ruin of their partners; while they regard the prostration of business, the distress among innocent classes and the destruction of great and honorable houses which they have wrought with an indifference as callous as if the sufferers were citizens of another planet."

And the *Nation* had a good deal to say about—

"the all but incredible prostitution of certain of our courts to the service of a notorious stock jobbing, gold gambling, railroad running and generally swindling clique." The conviction was growing that "courts are specially provided to give the strong and the wicked an opportunity to oppress the weak and the honest. . . . Already many business men feel ashamed to go to law. . . . Many respectable men will nowadays rather bear any loss short of absolute ruin than expose themselves to the disgrace of going into court. To sue has become almost equivalent to levying blackmail. To commence proceedings, for the justest of claims, is becoming disgraceful. It is getting honorable to be charged with the blackest of crimes."

There it was, but the most extraordinary part of it all, perhaps, was that Mr. Gould and Mr. Fisk remained friends. Of course the Erie was well worth a swallow or two of self-respect.

14

The Erie Railroad.

Mr. Gould was to have to do with many railroads—the Wabash, the Union Pacific, the Missouri Pacific, the Texas Pacific, the St. Louis and Northern, until in 1880 he controlled some ten thousand miles of track—and with several enterprises such as the Western Union and the Manhattan Elevated Railway. He was to be involved in some astonishing deals, Union Pacific, Kansas Pacific, Denver Pacific—public lands, coal lands, oil lands, "misappropriation of assets," "perjury and violence"—amounting to millions upon millions of dollars. He was to startle a not at all finicky financial world by the extent of his mercenary chicaneries, his ruthless manipulation and speculation, his profiteering in panic and in bankrutcy. He was to put one corporation after another, his own included, to the sack and pocket his profit, he was to subject himself to the accusation of having purposely ruined his own friends, he was to accumulate hatred and inspire industrial revolt through his merciless grinding down of wages. In a business era never surpassed for swindlery and brigandage, he was to have no equal.

It is unnecessary, perhaps, to attempt any detailed

enumeration of all this freebootery; more preferable to examine a series of transactions characteristic of the majority of his undertakings, of his methods and of his instincts—his dealings with the Erie Railroad.

It was in 1867; Mr. Drew was Treasurer, Mr. Gould and Mr. Fisk were directors; Mr. Vanderbilt was planning the consolidation of the Hudson River and Central roads, and, according to the New York *Times*—

> "Cornelius, the great Cornerer,
> A solemn oath he swore
> That in his trousers' pockets he
> Would put one railroad more;
> And when he swears he means it,
> The stout old Commodore."

To which Mr. Drew replied that—

> "Your bark is on the sea,
> But do not steer for Erie's Isle
> Since that's been struck by me.
> Go, man of sin, and leave me here
> To my theology!"

And the Erie War began.

15

The real cause of it, in the opinion of the New York *Herald,* was that—

"the Erie aroused the ire of the Vanderbilt party when it contracted to open a through broad gauge route to Chicago. . . . Here was threatened an independent line . . . which would . . . damage the Vanderbilt lines, and the [Vanderbilt] party at once plunged into litigation and afterwards into a huge stock jobbing operation in order to obtain control of the Erie."

But the Commodore went at it on the basis of reform. The Erie must be reformed. So he allied himself with a group of speculating Boston "reformers," promised them that he would oust Daniel Drew, secured their proxies and others in time for the annual election and found himself in a position to dispose of Mr. Drew. But Mr. Drew came whining to him and talked him out of it. The Boston gentlemen were told to mind their own business—one avoids a needless recital of strategic conferences—and Mr. Drew remained in the directorate, with Mr. Work as the Commodore's personal representative on the board. Whereupon, in February, 1868, Commodore Vanderbilt secured various injunctions, in particular restraining Mr. Drew and his fellow directors from issuing any more stock, from converting bonds into stock, and from executing any transactions in Erie securities pending the reimbursement of various sums appropriated in the past by Mr. Drew. And the Commodore began to purchase Erie stock.

It looked as though Mr. Drew were all tied up with injunctions, but Mr. Drew was a veritable eel. One cannot undertake in these pages any minute account of the complicated incidents related so fully by Mr. C. F. Adams and Mr. Moody; but before very long a secret meeting of the Erie executive committee—entirely disregarding the injunctions—had voted an issue of $10,000,000 of convertible bonds; Mr. Drew, Mr. Gould and Mr. Fisk had "converted" them and printed the corresponding stock certificates on their private printing press; the certificates had been ostensibly stolen by Mr. Fisk—actually, from the hands of a messenger boy, in order to safeguard them from further injunctions—and dumped onto a rising market in which Commodore Vanderbilt was industriously buying every share of Erie he could find; and Mr. Drew was in possession of an extraordinary collection of injunctions of his own, setting aside another judge's writs and forbidding Mr. Drew *not* to do what the Vanderbilt injunctions restrained him from doing.

It was, the New York *Nation* found,

"one of the most disgraceful prostitutions of legal forms ever witnessed, more like the tricks of the noisome creatures that infest the petty police courts. . . . The spectacle was witnessed of half a dozen judges at one and the same time issuing attachments and injunctions against plaintiffs and defendants, and against one another; lawyers and judges called out of their beds in the middle of the night, and respectable gentlemen waylaid in the street or hustled into their own doors to serve warrants upon them."

And on the Exchange the Vanderbilt brokers were wondering where all this Erie stock was coming from, but they obeyed their instructions to buy—until the news got around that Mr. Drew and his friends were printing certificates as fast as they could turn the crank, and the market crashed. Commodore Vanderbilt had been saddled with $7,000,000 of illegal Erie stock, $4,000,000 of which he had paid in greenbacks; there was very nearly a panic; and if the Commodore himself had not stood firm as a rock the bottom would have dropped out of Wall Street. Whatever his own sins, the old gentleman was always public spirited in a crisis. On this occasion, during the Black Friday days, in the panic of 1873, he did his best to maintain prices at personal sacrifice, he advanced money to forestall disaster, he was always a Bull.

A very angry Bull this time.

16

So that the next morning, March 11, the Erie directors were wanted for contempt of court, and, "anticipating a sudden visit of the officers of the law, a regular stampede took place . . . among the officials, each one lugging off an account book . . . or as many of the red tape documents as could be grasped," without forgetting the Commodore's greenbacks. In fact, "so complete a clearing out has not taken place," the *Herald* observed, "since the Fenians fled from Dublin." Or as the *Nation* saw it, the Erie directors stole away "like thieves . . . carrying with them millions of money." Through the fog, and across in the ferry to the Erie Offices in Jersey City, where they established themselves in the Ladies' Parlor of Taylor's Hotel. All but Mr. Fisk, who seems to have tarried in New York until a sheriff almost caught him, so that he was obliged to have himself rowed over to Jersey.

And then the Erie War began in earnest. With rumors of hired gangs, thugs, and "pugs," and "dead rabbits," coming to kidnap Mr. Drew—the Erie depot was thick with them on one occasion—the directors barricaded themselves in "Fort Taylor"; weapons and ammunition were assembled; twelve pounders were mounted on one of the docks; the Hudson County militia was held under arms while posses of citizens patrolled the streets; Mr. Fisk was put in charge of the "navy" which comprised "four small boats" filled with men armed with Springfield rifles; the whole place was packed with policemen, detectives and Erie "specials." Come one, come all

—and everybody very jumpy, and in particular Mr. Drew.

In the meantime the battle of injunctions continued, until one judge finally announced that he would rather run the risk of being fined than permit his court "to have anything to do with the scandal." It was, according to Mr. C. F. Adams, a "saturnalia of bench and bar," a panorama of "strange and revolting scenes," a "fearful exposé" of the current immorality and corruption of lawyers and judges, witnessed to its fullest degree in the court room of the amazing Judge Barnard. It was difficult, the *Nation* recorded—

"to state without indignation what an amount of depravity has been developed by these quarrels, but still more difficult to understand . . . the dense moral apathy, indifference, nay, the ghastly relish even, with which so much wickedness is generally regarded."

The community was drugged with fraud, it was acquiring the habit of venality, in the words of Henry Adams, it "stood helpless before the chaos."

17

And at Albany, around that Legislature which the New York *Independent* called "the worst assemblage of official thieves that ever disgraced the Capitol of the Empire State," the battle of bribery and subsidy raged between the two camps over the bill to legalize the recent issue of Erie stock, later referred to as the bill to "legalize counterfeit money." And at first the Vanderbilt funds were successful, and the bill was defeated, but Mr. Gould—under a cloud of injunctions and shepherded by sheriffs—arrived at the Develin House with reinforcements from the Erie treasury, and showers of gold began to inundate the lobbies of the Senate, where a similar bill was again being discussed. No one will ever know how much money was spent on the Senators, and Mr. Gould was always "perfectly astounded" when the word bribery was mentioned, but in April the bill was passed.

And two days later, when all this money stolen from the Erie was clinking in the pockets of the legislators, the terrible accident occurred, the "slaughter" of the burned car overturned down an embankment because of an old, defective rail. And perhaps Mr. Gould was "perfectly astounded" when he heard about that. As for the *Times,* it could only remark that—

"if the Erie Railroad managers should deem it for their interest to have a law passed sanctioning the recent slaughter and holding them free from all action in courts of law or elsewhere on account of it, we doubt not they could easily secure its passage by the Legislature."

And since the Senators had made their pile out of the bill, the members of the lower house were looking forward to a corresponding if not greater largesse from Mr. Gould, when suddenly, Mr. C. F. Adams writes, a "rumor ran through Albany as of some great public disaster, spreading panic and terror through hotel and corridor." And it was true. Commodore Vanderbilt had withdrawn his opposition and was making peace with Erie. There was to be no largesse for the members of the lower house.

The Erie directors had grown tired of sitting in Taylor's Hotel; the Commodore had spent enough money for the time being bribing legislators; the two parties came together. Secretly, it seems, with Mr. Gould and Mr. Fisk very suspicious at first of Mr. Drew, but they finally agreed on the terms. The contempt of court proceedings would be attended to; Commodore Vanderbilt was to be relieved of the Erie stock which had been dumped on him; Mr. Drew, Mr. Gould and Mr. Fisk were to keep their winnings from "short" sales of the stock; and Mr. Drew was to withdraw as a director of Erie, the road passing into the control of Mr. Gould and Mr. Fisk. An agreement involving payment of some $9,000,000 which were naturally taken from the Erie treasury.

"About twelve o'clock," Mr. Fisk testified later, "a paper was passed around and we signed it. . . .

I didn't read it . . . my impression is that I took my hat and left at once in disgust; I told Gould we had sold ourselves to the Devil. . . . I don't know what other documents I signed . . . after once the Devil had hold of me I kept on signing; didn't read any of them and have no idea what they were. . . . I went with the robbers then and I have been with them ever since."

Mr. Fisk was quite shocked by the whole transaction, and "thunderstruck and dumbfounded" by his fellow directors. And so was Mr. Gould. They protested virtuously that robbery was being committed —a belated scruple, surely—but there it was, the Devil had hold of them.

18

The Devil had hold of them, and they had hold of the Erie. In October, 1868, Mr. Gould was President, Mr. Tweed and his friend Peter Sweeney were elected directors, and a new era of inflation, corruption and speculation began. And now the trick was to clean out Daniel Drew.

The opportunity for the attempt was provided as the result of a transaction in greenbacks which came near precipitating a financial disaster as great as that of the subsequent Black Friday. Using the proceeds from the sale of a spurious issue of Erie shares, Mr. Drew, Mr. Gould and Mr. Fisk deposited in various banks some $14,000,000. Cheques were then drawn on those banks for the amounts deposited and presented simultaneously for payment in greenbacks. The object of this manipulation being, of course, to create a stringency of money causing a decline in shares so that the conspirators might profit by their heavy "short" sales of Erie. And one of the biggest Bears was that "wealthy gentleman of advanced years, of eminent piety, a builder of churches, a founder of colleges, a former Treasurer of the Erie Company," Mr. Drew.

The effect of suddenly withdrawing such a sum in greenbacks from the bank reserve was, as the *Nation* put it, "electrical." The banks called in their loans, money "became almost unobtainable, and whoever had borrowed money on stocks was compelled to sell to pay off his loans. . . . Trade throughout the country was brought to a perfect standstill. . . . It required the strong arm of the Treasury to prevent the panic from spreading all over the country." Stocks crashed, and Mr. Gould and Mr. Fisk "purchased almost all the shares of Erie that were in the market," and many "short" contracts, *"notably the contracts of the former Treasurer of the road."*

Never, the *Nation* thought—

"was a bolder scheme planned. . . . By a fraudulent over issue of stock these men had depressed the price

"RUINED"

From a woodcut in *Harper's Weekly* inspired by Black Friday

of Erie stock . . . reaping an enormous profit; and with the money so obtained they had run up the price of gold and made another large profit; they had then again advanced the price of Erie . . . and made a larger profit than ever. In the course of these operations they had ruined hundreds . . . had arrested the whole business of the country . . . had brought the banks to the verge of suspension and seriously threatened the national credit."

It was this little episode which President Grant seemed to have forgotten during the months preceding Black Friday. And in order to safeguard themselves, these Erie directors had obtained an injunction restraining themselves, and appointing themselves receivers and custodians of the funds enjoined—an "outrageous caricature of justice."

But Mr. Drew had "attempted to betray their schemes." He had been frightened by the uproar and had withdrawn from the greenback affair, so that Mr. Fisk called him "Turn Tail" and "Danny Cold Feet." But Mr. Drew had continued confidingly to sell Erie "short," and before Mr. Drew knew where he was his two friends who had turned Bulls had him cornered. In the midst of another tornado of injunctions Mr. Drew went to Mr. Gould and Mr. Fisk to ask for time on his contracts, and was laughed at and told that "he was the last man who ought to whine over any position in which he has placed himself in regard to Erie." There was no Erie stock to be had, for Mr. Gould and Mr. Fisk had secured Judge Barnard's permission to buy back the fraudulent issue—with Erie funds—at any price up to par regardless of the lower price at which it had originally been sold, on the plea that the issue had been illegal! A performance which "all good men" should brand as "infamous," the *Nation* kept shouting.

It was a magnificent corner, contrived in defiance of several injunctions and a corporation law of the State of New York, but Mr. Gould and Mr. Fisk had miscalculated. Some of the shares of a special English issue had been sold in America, and with Erie soaring these shares began to appear on the market. In the last five minutes of time Mr. Drew was able to make his deliveries, at a loss of perhaps half a million dollars.

But he had the consolation of seeing Mr. Gould and Mr. Fisk lose several millions in consequence of the broken corner, and all three of them had the pleasure of reading in the *Nation* that—

"the management of the Erie Railroad Company has for years past been sought by the most unscrupulous gamblers and rogues that the financial history of the world has any record of. The men who at the last election of directors . . . succeeded in obtaining the control . . . have so far surpassed their last predecessors in villany as their last predecessors had already surpassed any that had gone before them; and their exploits during the last few weeks have brought to light . . . such deep seated judicial corruption, and so low a fall in the pervading tone of commercial morality, that the calmest spectator stands by in amazement and can only wonder when retribution will begin."

19

Perhaps one might as well leave it there. Astounding corruption, farcical injunctions, spurious receiverships, illegal issues of stock, incredible inflation—Mr. Gould's theory that it was necessary to issue new stock all the time in order to preserve the Erie from falling into Commodore Vanderbilt's hands; the increasing of the road's capitalization by some $60,000,000 in eight years; the looting of the Erie treasury so as to provide funds for the "India rubber" bribery account; the appropriation by Mr. Gould of some $12,000,000 of his company's money, estimated by the Hepburn investigating committee; the famous "classification act" under which Mr. Gould and Mr. Fisk made themselves directors for five years; the Erie offices garrisoned with detectives, besieged by process servers—the recital of these transactions would simply furnish an accumulating and redundant chronicle of fearsome speculation, of revolting dishonesty, of superlative profiteering.

Throughout the whole shameful business, the most

distressing circumstance is to be found, surely, in the public apathy which could permit the continuance for years of so conspicuous a disgrace. One may condemn Mr. Gould, but one cannot absolve a community, a Federal administration, a generation so crassly tolerant of depravity.

"There is too much truth," the *Nation* deplored, "in the statement that the tendency today in this country is to count up our list of peculiarly American virtues as consisting of audacity, push, unscrupulousness and brazen disregard of others' rights or others' good opinions; that we make no sufficient objection to a display of unmitigated and unmitigable selfishness, if only it be a splendid display—if only it be crowned by success, by the acquisition of wealth or power."

The nation was very sick.

They got rid of him finally—the stockholders whose pockets were being picked. Led by the English stockholders and General Sickles, they sued him, and in 1874 he agreed to restore $6,000,000 and to retire from the Erie provided all pending suits against him should be dropped. And because he knew that Erie stock would rise as soon as he resigned—there could be no better piece of news from Erie than that it had freed itself of his calamitous presence—he bought as much as he could beforehand. And the real estate and securities which went to make up the $6,000,-

000 were found afterwards to be worth actually only some $200,000. It was the Devil, no doubt, who still had hold of Mr. Gould.

He was an extraordinary little man with an amazing memory for names and faces. A thin, bilious, swarthy, silent, heavily bearded, rather Jewish appearing little man with shrinking ways and slightly effeminate manners, who seldom looked with his staring, steely eyes at the person to whom he was speaking. His private life was irreproachable; except for his beautifully appointed railroad car and his yacht *Atalanta,* he was not ostentatious; he had a lovely home at Irvington filled with works of art, in his stables were many carriages and horses, and his conservatories were celebrated. He was a very great lover of flowers, a botanist of merit, an eager collector of orchids.

He was generous more frequently than was supposed, and Mrs. Fisk was to write after her husband's death that Mr. Gould was "the only friend of Mr. Fisk who has responded to my actual needs and wants.... He never has proved unmindful to the needs of those deserving his charity." Men who worked for him are said to have been devoted to him; although Edward Bok, who at the age of eighteen served him for a while as confidential stenographer and once made use of his tips on the market, found that "the closer his contact with Jay Gould the more doubtful he became of the wisdom of such an association and perhaps its unconscious influence upon his own life in its formative period." And "Edward Bok's instinct," Mr. Bok records, "never failed him. He felt that his path lay far apart from that of Jay Gould—and the farther the better."

A curious little man—Jay Gould—with his personal sensibility, his private charity and his flowers; and outside of his home, beyond his domestic circles, endowed with "courage, grit, insight, foresight, tireless energy, indomitable will"; armed with an impenetrable contempt of public opinion—no hypocrite ever, for "he never stooped to hypocrisy. . . . He bought many things, but he never bought a eulogy. He played the great game of speculative finance for all it could be made to yield without disguise or apology"—a stranger to honesty and good faith; a personality of alarming cunning deprived of all feeling, scornful of any consideration of rectitude. An "operator" who always "played with loaded dice"; an administrator whose only interest lay in the accumulation of selfish profits; a genius whose talents were completely devoted to the limited spheres of his own enrichment; a parasite of disaster, an instrument of calamity, a destroyer. A collector of orchids, that sinister flower—himself the most lurid blossom nurtured in the poisonous swamps, in the infected shadows of the financial jungle of his day.

A timid little man who always took his pound of flesh. And men were always threatening him, trying to get at him to kill him; maniacs, fanatics, unfortunates who proclaimed that he had ruined them, shabby individuals who spoke of themselves as victims; he had to have a bodyguard and traffic with detectives. During his last years he suffered from dyspepsia and insomnia. And on December 2, 1892, leaving $72,-000,000 to his sons and daughters, he died of consumption and mental strain. And when it was announced, the stocks of all his corporations rose in a rejoicing market.

Jim Fisk
The Mountebank

JIM FISK

THE MOUNTEBANK

1

"A DOG is an animal with fore legs because he is a quadrooped. . . . The bulldog is the best fighting dog because most likely he was made for that purpus. . . . I think the newfoundland is the noblest dog, he saves children from drownding and they are sagasious. This is all for the present."

These interesting observations were inscribed in a copybook of the 1840s by the boy, Jim Fisk; the big, rollicking, good-natured Green Mountain boy of Brattleboro who was later to be called Colonel and Admiral, Prince Erie and Jim Jubilee, and some of whose financial exploits in the company of Daniel Drew and Jay Gould have already invited a considerable attention in preceding pages.

"My business," he once testified—he was to do a great deal of testifying during his life—"my business is railroading, steamboating, and I suppose I may add speculating." A modest statement from the man who was Comptroller of the Erie Railroad prior to its regeneration, who commanded the "navy" at Fort Taylor during the "Erie War," who enjoyed the privilege of partnership with Jay Gould and of intimacy with the Tweed Ring, and who was the dark angel of the Black Friday gold panic.

Cornelius Vanderbilt, Jay Gould, Daniel Drew, Jim Fisk—posterity has remembered only the first two because of the fortunes which they bequeathed, and has forgotten bankrupt Danny and spendthrift Jim; but in the brief day of his diamond studded importance there was perhaps no man better known in America than Jim Fisk; at the moment of his violently dramatic end, the news of his death, one learns from a contemporary account, "flew on wings of light" and found international prominence in the columns of European newspapers; at the present time, the man to whom Henry Ward Beecher referred as "that supreme mountebank of fortune" remains unchallenged as an exhibit of the success and popularity which a generous, shrewd, energetic, corrupt and altogether native vulgarity could achieve in the post civil war period of American financial life.

He was a big, burly, blond creature with "kiss curls" who looked like a butcher, jovial and quick witted, with the manners and gaudy habits of a publican; he was a swindler and a bandit, a destroyer of law and an apostle of fraud; he was a clown in velvet waistcoats and spurious admiral's uniforms, a fatuous fat man who never grew up, playing with railroads and steamboats, canary birds and *ballerinas;* his private life was to many a public dismay, his public conduct to some a private scorn; he was, for a while, the most successful, the most conspicuous, the most significant figure in the sinister business world of New York. And to hundreds of his fellow citizens—thousands, as was shown when his funeral train passed by—he was charitable, light hearted, open handed big Jim Fisk; a community which loathed Jay Gould adored him; and when he died they honored him with ballads. The America of the Sixties produced him, and nowhere perhaps, except in the America of 1870, could he have existed.

2

He was born in 1834, at Bennington in Vermont, the son of James Fisk, a country peddler. Removed at an early age to Brattleboro—where his father built and spasmodically managed the Revere House in which the boy himself at one time worked as a waiter —he grew up under the care of a stepmother whom he remembered in his will, attended the district school without enthusiasm and endeared himself to everyone as a bright, fun loving, handy youngster, fond of horses and dogs, and of little children.

Except for an interlude during which he travelled with Van Amburgh's circus, as a sweeper first and later as ticket collector, he accompanied his father on his peddling trips; but the parent methods were too conservative for young Jim. He wanted gaudy carts like the circus wagons, and glittering harness, and fast Blackhawk horses with which to drive furiously through gaping villages distributing pennies and candy to the children. And when his father hesitated Jim started out alone and became a "jobber in silks, shawls, dress goods, jewelry, silver ware and Yankee notions"; and soon he had several carts covering various routes, and the money rolled in, and he bought out his father. It was the painted circus carts, and the dashing horses, and the smiling, blarneying Jim that did the trick. Always gay, and generous, and jaunty. Always conspicuous. The circus man.

He did so well that the Boston firm of Jordan and Marsh from whom he bought his goods offered him a position as a salesman in their store. But Jim was not made for a counter jumper; he hated the work and he was a failure—when the Civil War broke out. The Government must have blankets; Jordan and Marsh had a great many fine old blankets in their loft; there was in Boston, it was said, a lady who had influence with Congressmen. Jim Fisk met the lady, Jordan and Marsh obtained the blanket contract. Jim Fisk went to Washington; he entertained, he made himself pleasant; Jordan and Marsh obtained other contracts. At Jim Fisk's suggestion

JAMES FISK, JR.

they bought several mills and began manufacturing their own goods at an enormous profit. Soon he was a partner.

Not long afterwards they were begging him to resign, for a consideration. He was filling the whole place, crowding them out; and there was a little alleged matter of cotton smuggling which alarmed them, in spite of his energetic organizing of Boston's relief for the wounded. This citizen was becoming too prominent, this partner too successful. He opened a store of his own, but the times were wrong and he failed. In 1864 he went to New York, to Wall Street, to be a broker. In a short time he was ruined.

"Wall Street has ruined me," he said, "and Wall Street shall pay for it." It did.

He went back to Boston for a while—there was a wife there, Lucy Moore of Springfield, an ample lady who mothered him and who does not intrude in any degree upon his chronicle—and in time he was back in New York with a scheme for selling the Stonington Steamboat Line which Daniel Drew was anxious to unload. The scheme was successful, Uncle Daniel sensed a kindred freebooting spirit, and young Jim Fisk was set up in business with another protégé—Mr. Belden, the son of a "camp meeting shouter"—to serve as Uncle Daniel's private broker in the forthcoming Erie fracas which has already been described in these pages, and which was eventually to place Jim Fisk in the Erie directorate and Uncle Daniel out of it.

It was then, in the late Sixties, that Wall Street began to pay.

3

It is not intended here to recapitulate Jim Fisk's dealings with Jay Gould and with the Erie, or even to discuss his performance with the Albany and Susquehanna—an incredible episode of telegraphic injunctions and rival trains charging each other on a disputed track, during the course of which Mr. Fisk saw himself thrown downstairs and out onto an Albany sidewalk. However extraordinary his business activities, he was never so astonishing in his office as out of it.

For instance, his colonelcy. The estimable Ninth Regiment, N.Y.S.N.G., was heavily in debt; Mr. Fisk paid all the bills and in April, 1870, was elected receiver—Colonel, rather. There followed some magnificent moments. A moonlight parade up Fifth Avenue, behind the famous band, led by the resplendent Colonel. Of course the Lieutenant Colonel gave all the orders. A summer encampment at "Camp Gould" at Long Branch, where the Colonel had a house; a perspiring business, complicated by frequent desertions in search of beer, but they drilled, and the

Colonel perhaps hardest of all. Only no other regiment appeared to escort them when they came back, and there had been some mortification over a ball which did not turn out so well socially. Then a trip to Boston, for the anniversary of Bunker Hill. The City of Boston said certainly not, and called it "a new era in the history of effrontery"; but the Governor of Massachusetts gave his consent to this invasion of the state and the gallant Ninth paraded through "the Athens of America," and gave a concert on the Common, and in general had the best of the argument. It was a *very* good band, in red coats.

And then a terrible affair the following summer. The riot attendant upon the parade of the Orangemen. The militia, including the Ninth, were called out, and behaved in an idiotically indiscriminate manner with loaded muskets, with the result that a great many people were killed and wounded. And in the midst of it all, the Colonel of the Ninth was hit by a chunk of iron and ran away. As the poem in *Harper's Weekly* had it—

> "Jim Fisk arose from dreams of wrath,
> In purple dyed sublimity,
> And took his usual morning bath
> With soap and equanimity.
> Then girding him for cruel war,
> He buckled round his puny form
> His bright, expensive cimetar,
> And donned his first class uniform."

But there was a disagreeable commotion outside, and—

> "Without his hat, without his sword,
> He rushed into the thick of it,
> Till in a moment he was floored,
> And very, very sick of it.
> His comrades coming to his aid,
> And finding him quite quakery,
> His manly person straight conveyed
> To a convenient bakery . . . "

And when the mob came clamoring after him to lynch him he departed from the bakery across back lots; changed his regimentals for some haphazard garments picked up on the way; found himself in a fortunate cab with Jay Gould being conveyed to the Hoffman House; and retreated thence again to the more remote security of Long Branch.

Still, a few months later, he died courageously of painful wounds, and was taken to his grave under the battle flag of the Ninth.

4

When he was not parading as a Colonel, Mr. Fisk enjoyed being an Admiral. His sale of the Stonington Line had brought him in contact with steamboat interests, and in 1869 he became president of the Narragansett Steamship Company, operating splendidly luxurious three deckers down the Sound out of

Bristol. The *Providence* and the *Bristol*—bronzes, mirrors, gildings, brass bands—marine circus wagons.

And until the novelty wore off the showman was there every afternoon at the pier in New York to see them start—"in a full Admiral's uniform of the finest make," with a "huge diamond sparkling in his shirt bosom," taking his place at the gangway "where he must be seen by all who entered." And on some occasions he was attended by "his female favorite of the hour, attired [in] a jacket of navy blue with gilt buttons and epaulettes, a hat in the sailor style, and decked out in all matters of detail in a manner evidently indicating a careful consultation of the Admiral's taste." Pierrot and Columbine.

The climax of this mood was achieved in June, 1869, when Admiral Fisk conveyed President Grant to Newport in one of his steamboats and accompanied him to Boston for the Peace Jubilee. An extraordinary musical festival in a coliseum seating fifty thousand auditors, involving an orchestra of one thousand pieces, a choir of ten thousand voices, an "anvil chorus" manipulated by one hundred firemen in red shirts, a great chime of bells and a battery of Parrott guns controlled by electricity. General Grant is said to have greatly enjoyed the guns. As for "Jim Jubilee," there was "nothing the matter with *my* old tin stove," as he was so fond of saying when things were going well for him. Sixty thousand people to look at him while he followed the President down the aisle. He was in his full Admiral's uniform, bowing and smiling in reply to cheers which it did not occur to him might be intended for Admiral Farragut, and "for simple sensation his presence . . . quite surpassed that of General Grant." The supreme mountebank.

In 1870 he had to have a new toy, and it was the *Plymouth Rock* for the Sandy Hook and Long Branch summer traffic; fitted out with "thirty-two suites of apartments that rival New York's finest hotel for elegance and comfort," the furnishings "surpassing in profusion and luxuriance anything to be met with by a traveler anywhere else in the world." The bar was "of a size and elegance rarely equalled in any establishment on *terra firma,* being extensively finished in white marble, with large mirrors and all the usual appurtenances." A very "extensive" steamer in every way.

And in every saloon and cabin the Admiral put canary birds in gilded cages. One of them was named Jay Gould.

5

At the same time Mr. Fisk fancied himself as an impresario. He not only rebuilt the Fifth Avenue Theatre and managed it for a while, as well as the

Academy of Music, but he bought Pike's Opera House on Twenty-third Street and turned it into a glittering, three hundred thousand dollar white marble palace for the production of French opera. His greatest success seems to have been *The Twelve Temptations*, a spectacular piece with a tremendous ballet in which blondes and brunettes appeared on alternate evenings. In his opera-bouffes he sometimes sent on a different cast in each act. Entire troupes were imported from France, one famous *ballerina* after another graced his boards, internationally known conductors argued, and on occasions fought with him. He lost enormous sums of money.

It was for this reason, perhaps—or simply because he preferred to be near his ballet girls, and only a few steps away from his own house—that he caused the offices of the Erie Railroad to be moved, and installed at the Opera House. The most fantastic offices ever occupied by a business corporation—a splendor of marble, and black walnut inlaid with gold, and silver name plates, and crimson hangings, and painted ceilings, and washstands decorated with nymphs and cupids—in the midst of which Prince Erie throned in his corpulent shirtsleeves, pushing buttons, ordering injunctions from Judge Barnard and, not infrequently, opening champagne and oysters for the gay ladies of the opera, while Jay Gould sat timidly in his corner thinking of his orchids and deploring the blatancies of his cabbage plant of a partner.

His railroad, his steamboat line, his regiment, his opera, his six black and white horses, his lovely ladies—big Jim was so fond of his toys, his "old tin stove" was in such splendid shape, life was such a magnificent circus. He had so many conspicuous parts to play, so much money to throw out of the windows, such "nobby" velvet waistcoats, and gold braided uniforms, and dazzling diamond studs to wear. Lucy Fisk was distantly majestic in her Newport villa, affectionately tolerant of her mountebank's antics. In New York, right there on Twenty-third Street, there was the beautiful Josie "Dollie" who loved her James, and called him Sardines.

6

Helen Josephine Mansfield, a "voluptuous" woman. She was in her twenties, tall with dark hair and "very large and lustrous eyes," and a "pearly white skin"; the divorced wife of the actor Frank Lawler. A native of Boston, she had come to New York from California, secured an introduction to Mr. Fisk and accepted his lavish attentions at a time when she was herself destitute. Carriages, horses, diamonds, servants, an "elegant domicile" on Twenty-third Street—in which Judge Barnard once consented to hold court—but it was not enough, and in 1870 Josie and Jim were quarreling over money matters.

That was one reason; another was his promiscuous enthusiasm for the ladies of the ballet; still another her own for Ned Stokes. Mr. Stokes had had dealings in oil with Mr. Fisk, he was handsome, elegant, socially prominent; the two men were great friends; Josie was at home to both of them. Pierrot Jim was losing his Columbine. At first he hoped that they might meet again "where the woodbine twineth, over the river Jordan, on the bright and beautiful banks of Heaven." Later on he still had a few pictures of her, "but they have found a place among the nothings which fill the waste basket under my table." As for Ned Stokes, "cling to him; be careful what you do for he will be watchful. How well he knows you cheated me. He will look for the same." But not long afterwards Mr. Fisk was sending her money again, and pleading with her to give up Mr. Stokes, and complaining tearfully that "she don't even let me leave my gum shoes in the house."

In the meantime there is no doubt that Mr. Fisk was doing his best to ruin Mr. Stokes. Whether or not he threatened, as was afterwards alleged, to "put him out of the way"—it could easily be arranged for five hundred dollars Mr. Fisk was supposed to have said—he found plenty of legal opportunities to harass his rival. Mr. Stokes was arrested on a charge of embezzlement; when he retaliated with an accusation of conspiracy his Erie oil contracts were cancelled; the battle went on in a suit of Mr. Stokes's for two hundred thousand dollars' damages. And suddenly Josie saw fit to give Mr. Stokes all of Mr. Fisk's letters for publication. The mountebank could not bear to be made ridiculous. A settlement was arrived at; Mr. Fisk paid fifteen thousand dollars and the letters were placed in the hands of Peter Sweeney, the arbitrator.

Mr. Fisk immediately charged Mr. Stokes and Josie with blackmail; their counter libel and perjury suit came up for trial late in 1871, in the Yorkville police court. Mr. Fisk appeared in a short navy jacket "ornamented by a multitude of gold buttons of various sizes and shapes" bearing the monogram of the Narragansett Steamship Company; Mr. Stokes had his hair "crimped"; Josie's "delicate hands were encased in faultless lavender kid gloves," and on her head was "perched a jaunty little Alpine hat with a dark green feather." There were two postponements, and on the morning of Saturday, January 6, 1872, another hearing, somewhat mortifying for the hot tempered Mr. Stokes, took place. Mr. Fisk was not present.

A good deal of confusion exists concerning what occurred after the court adjourned. Mr. Fisk is said to have visited Josie to offer her a compromise, then for a while he was at the Opera House. Mr. Stokes lunched at Delmonico's with his lawyers. There, apparently, a rumor reached him that the Grand Jury had indicted him for blackmail. He seems to have gone to see Josie, and driven slowly past the Opera House, gazing at the Erie office windows.

At about four o'clock in the afternoon Mr. Fisk passed through the ladies' entrance of the Grand Central Hotel and started up the side stairway to call on a young lady, the daughter of an old friend. A few moments later he was found at the bottom of the stairs. He had been shot twice, once through the arm and again through the abdomen. He was taken upstairs to the room in which some seventeen hours later he died in the presence of his wife and brothers-in-law, while Mr. Gould, and Mr. Tweed, and various other associates waited in an adjoining parlor.

In the lobby of the hotel shots had been heard; a man who had come down the main stairway was seen running towards the barber shop exit; after a commotion he was seized. It was Ned Stokes. Mr. Fisk, who was in complete possession of his faculties, identified him before the Coroner as the man who had fired at him from the landing. At the inquest Mr. Fisk's doctors testified that they had found no weapons on his person. None were found in the hallway, only Mr. Stokes's pistol which he had thrown under a sofa on the floor above.

In the face of Mr. Stokes's plea of *self defence* which carried him through three trials—from a disagreement to an appealed conviction, and thence to a final verdict of manslaughter in the third degree—one hesitates further to specify the details of an event to which there were no reliable immediate witnesses. The official decision of a jury prevents discussion of the timeliness of Mr. Stokes's presence on the landing of the ladies' stairway; forbids repetition of contemporary assertions, however well informed, concerning certain private aspects of the case.

7

Jim Jubilee was dead; his "old tin stove" was out. "The poor Erie Prince"—one quotes from a young southern lady's unpublished diary—

"has himself 'gone where the woodbine twineth'. . . Poor fellow, he was only thirty-seven years old, and had risen . . . to [be] one of the most noted men of the age. Now that he is dead numberless anecdotes are told of his generosity and kind heartedness, and the feeling of sorrow for his death is universal."

Or perhaps not quite, since from the illuminating words of another contemporary one learns that—

"as a rule actresses, ballet girls and adventuresses on the one hand, and the higher order of truly Chris-

COLONEL JAMES FISK, JR.
From the cover of the *Ninth Regiment Quickstep*

JIM FISK

tian women on the other, seem disposed . . . to look upon the late speculator with emotions of kindness and pity; but the large, orthodox, reputable, domestic, home loving, middle class of females . . . regard the departed with the same aversion in death as in life."

Still, thousands of people came to see his military lying in state at the Opera House, including great numbers of females. Twenty-third Street was packed, the roofs and windows black with spectators. One ventures to note the "simple incident" of the barber, Charlie, who twirled the deceased's blond moustache, exclaiming "one more twirl, dearest of friends, for the last time." The cortège got under way, finally, up Fifth Avenue to the railroad "depot." The crowd, one reads in the diary, was—

"dense, literally packing the sidewalks . . . and all the windows were full of people. First came one hundred of the police, then the band of the Ninth Regiment . . . and then another band. . . . Then came the Ninth Regiment, all with crepe on their arms. . . . Then there were the officers of the brigade . . . followed by the hearse drawn by six horses . . . and then came crowds of citizens on foot and an immense number of carriages. It was altogether one of the most imposing sights I ever saw. The papers report that the coffin was of rosewood with gold mountings, and that he was buried in his [Colonel's] uniform."

All along the route of the funeral train the depots were crammed with people; two thousand at Bridgeport, three thousand at New Haven, enormous crowds at Hartford and Springfield, hundreds on the platform of every little station. At midnight they were at Brattleboro, carrying him to the Revere House. At the lying in state in the Baptist Church he had a white "boquet" in one hand, his military cap in the other; the Reverend Jenkins prayed thirty harrowing minutes for Mr. Fisk, for his family, for his regiment, for Brattleboro and for the United States; the service closed in a clamor of hysterics. They buried him in that cemetery of which he had said, not long before, that it did not require a new fence, since "those in couldn't get out, and those out didn't want to get in!"

There was talk of a monument with figures to represent Commerce, Railroads, Navigation and the Drama.

8

The mountebank was in his grave, and immediately, except perhaps for the "home loving, middle class of females," plain people forgot his clowning—

the irregularities, too, of his personal conduct and of his business habits—and remembered only that he had been frank, and goodnatured, and helping. A bighearted fellow in shirtsleeves. They recalled his ready charity at the time of the Chicago fire; began suddenly to recite the unsuspected roll of his lavish private kindnesses. No one had ever been turned away. He was the poor man's friend. It did not matter about Black Friday, and the Erie, and Josie Mansfield; along the sidewalks of New York they missed his big laugh, the quick, unostentatious generosity of his big, diamond flashing hands—and a song was written. A song about big Jim whom they had loved.

He was, they thought, a man "who wore his heart on his sleeve, no matter what people would say; and he did all his deeds, both the good and the bad, in the broad open light of the day"; and so—

"Let me speak of a man who's now dead in his grave,
  A good man as ever was born;
  Jim Fisk he was called, and his money he gave
  To the outcast, the poor and forlorn.
  We all know he loved both women and wine,
  But his heart it was right I am sure;
  Though he lived like a prince in a palace so fine,
  Yet he never went back on the poor!
  If a man was in trouble Fisk helped him along
  To drive the grim wolf from the door;
  He strove to do right, though he may have done wrong,
  But he never went back on the poor!"

Cornelius Vanderbilt had his statue, Jay Gould his orchids. Jim Fisk had none of these, but he had his ballad. He would not have complained; he would, on the contrary, most certainly have insisted that there was nothing the matter with *his* old tin stove.

www.ingramcontent.com/pod-product-compliance
Lightning Source LLC
Chambersburg PA
CBHW020646230426
43665CB00008B/333